AMERICA'S SPECIAL FORCES

David Bohrer

MBI Publishing Company

First published in 2002 by MBI Publishing Company, Galtier Plaza, Suite 200, 380 Jackson Street, St. Paul, MN 55101-3885 USA

MBI Publishing Company books are also available at discounts in bulk quantity for industrial or sales-promotional use. For details write to Special Sales Manager at Motorbooks International Wholesalers & Distributors, Galtier Plaza, Suite 200, 380 Jackson Street, St. Paul, MN 55101-3885 USA.

Library of Congress Cataloging-in-Publication Data Available.

ISBN 0-7603-1348-2

On the front cover: U.S. Army Rangers advance through a trench and bunker system at Fort Lewis during a 12-day battalion movement and evaluation exercise. To maintain a high level of readiness, Rangers are constantly working on their skills. Each battalion can deploy anywhere in the world in 18 hours or less.

On the frontispiece: Navy SEAL high altitude parachute equipment, which consists of a helmet, oxygen tanks, mask, and MT-1X parachute. Jump training for SEALs and all other special operations forces is one of the few centralized schools. Static-line training is done at Ft. Benning, Georgia, while all other initial jump training in done in Yuma, Arizona.

On the title page: America's highly trained special forces are experts at approaching by stealth, achieving their objectives, and slipping silently away. They often overcome overwhelming odds by exploiting the element of suprise.

On the back cover, top: A view of the Mark V Special Operations Craft (SOC) as it speeds across the open ocean at 50 knots. The high performance craft is designed to carry a crew of 16 SEALs or other Special Operations Forces for medium range insertion or extraction. It has a crew of five, a range in excess of 600 nautical miles, and is sized to permit air deployment aboard a C-5 aircraft.

On the back cover, bottom: A Navy SEAL decked out in high altitude parachute equipment, consisting of a helmet, oxygen tanks, mask, and MT-1X parachute. Special forces are often deployed by parachute at night from high altitude so they can glide in several miles towards their unsuspecting objective.

Edited by Mike Haenggi
Designed by Katie L. Sonmor

Printed in China

CONTENTS

ACKNOWLEDGMENTS

The world of U.S. Special Operations is not a large one. Although their members are but a handful of the nation's military might, their impact on our lives and way of life is immeasurable. Most of their actions we will never know. Most of their contributions we will never read about. When a special operator is lost in the line of duty, their memory goes largely unreported. It is the price of secrecy and the result of the career they have chosen. The people within this community are unquestionable examples of "unsung heroes."

This book could not have been made without the cooperation and contributions of these people. From the many public affairs officers and civilians who work so hard to publicize a community whose very nature is to avoid publicity, to the special operators themselves who allowed me into their world to photograph their work, I owe a great deal of thanks. I would especially like to extend my sincere thanks to the following individuals:

David Viens and Jeff Notte of Eastman Kodak Co., for their support and generous sponsorship of this project, for providing all of the Kodak film for this project, and for seeing it to completion. Additionally, to David Alexander and the staff of A&I Color Lab in Hollywood, California, for their invaluable support and quality color processing and color printing services.

My thanks to the talented photographers and editors at the *Los Angeles Times, Valley Edition*, whom I have always held in high regard, along with Managing Editor Steve Padilla, and Photo Editor Steve Stroud, who so graciously allotted me leave of absence, and words of encouragement, to complete this project.

To my friends and associates who helped me constantly throughout the production of this book—Frank Esposito, Robert Martinez, Brian VanderBrug, Jill Connelly, David Butow, Todd Bigelow, Gerard Burkhart, Richard Derk, Mark Savage, David Muronaka, George Wilhelm, Rolando Otero, Julie Markes, Donna Hagen, Joan Cassese, Joe and Sandra DeMeo, Bob Crosby, Matt Randall, Kari-Rene Hall, Bob Mroz, Gia Castiglia, Julie Castiglia, Chuck Bennett, Dr. Alan Salvi, Sandy "Sandra Beth" Salvi-Trebra, Kim Janecek, Melinda Manning, Mr. Orange, Matthew Harrington, Claire Vitucci, Lori Cohen, Judith Campbell, Vanessa Hillian, Akili Ramsess, and John McCoy.

A special thanks to Raliegh Souther for the tireless hours spent with me editing through the thousands of images produced during the span of this project.

In addition, my thanks to the many extraordinary and interesting individuals of the U.S. military with whom I had the opportunity to meet and work closely with during the production of this book. Their contributions and assistance made this work possible:

Col.Robert E. Pilnacek and George B. Grimes, Public Affairs, U.S. Special Operations Command at MacDill AFB, Florida

Rear Admiral Thomas R. Richards and Lt. Commander James R. Fallin of the U.S. Naval Special Warfare Command in Coronado, California.

Gen. Wayne A. Downing, U.S. Army (retired), former Commander-in-Chief, USSOCOM.

Paul Nelson, U.S. Army Special Warfare Center and School Public Affairs Office.

Lt. Col. Walter E. Pierce, Carol Jones, Maj. Andrew J. Lucas, and Capt. Cabot Gatlin of the U.S. Army Special Operations Command Public Affairs Office.

Capt. Robert Matthews, U.S. Army 7th Special Forces Group

The members of the U.S. Army National Guard 133rd Public Affairs Detatchment.

Lt. Megan Mason, Lt. Brian Gobel, U.S. Marine Corps Public Affairs Office, Camp Pendleton, California.

Lt. Col. James Thomas, 1st Force Reconnassaince Unit, U.S. Marine Corps.

Col. Steve Cheney, Maj. Katie Haddock, and SSgt. Charlotte "Charlie" Crouch, U.S. Marine Corps Recruit Depot, San Diego, California.

Sherry Suhosky, U.S. Marine Corps (retired), president of the USMC Combat Correspondents Association.

Maj. Nancy LaLuntas, U.S. Marine Corps Public Affairs Office, Los Angeles, California.

Maj. Matthew Durham, Shirley Sikes, and 1st Lt. Darren Berry of the U.S. Air Force Special Operations Command, Public Affairs Office, Hurlburt Field, Florida, for their assistance in organizing for me Operation Massive Interference, and to the pilots and members of the Air Force 16th Special Operations Wing who participated.

And again, moreover, to all the members of the U.S. Special Operations community who had a hand in educating me, assisting me, and allowing me into their world in order for this book to be produced.

A special thanks to Timothy Williams, whose writing made this book an accurate and telling portrayal of a community often shrouded in secrecy.

In addition, a personal thanks must be extended to my editor, Mike Haenggi at Motorbooks International, who astonishingly seemed to never grow tired of my constant phone calls, and worked tirelessly with me to see this difficult project to a conclusion.

And most of all, to Randy Leffingwell, an author and photographer whose talent is matched only by his personal kindness and passion for his work. His patience and encouragement—and introduction of Matthew Harrington's Doomsday principle—helped me immensely in multiple periods of adversity.

This book is dedicated to my mom and dad, whose love and devotion have supported and encouraged me to do what I want, rather than what I need.

David Bohrer

INTRODUCTION

Sometimes it takes only a glance to discern the individuals who belong to America's Special Operations teams from those in regular military units. They are the ones who appear older and have a look of supreme confidence in their eyes and their step. They have become known as "The Quiet Professionals."

Special operators do the deeds that no one else dares. The Air Force has Special Tactics teams, Pararescue, and the pilots and crews who fly a myriad of Special Operations aircraft. In the Army, it is the Rangers, Special Forces, 160th Special Operations Aviation Regiment, psychological operations groups, Civil Affairs, and the super-secret Delta Force. The Navy has the SEALs and Special Boat units; and the Marines have Force Reconnaissance units. Generally these groups share the same goals. They sneak behind enemy lines, assault well-defended enemy military bases and airfields, and rescue soldiers and hostages. They are called upon when diplomacy fails and political or military considerations rule out the deployment of a larger conventional force.

Though they are members of their respective services, each, apart from the Marines, works for the U.S. Special Operations Command (USSOCOM), which in many cases reports directly to the National Command Authority (NCA)—the president, the secretary of defense, the Joint Chiefs of Staff. There are about 47,000 members of USSOCOM, composed of both active and reserve personnel located at bases in the United States and overseas.

In the post-Cold War world, a world in which the threat of Soviet attack has dissipated and more attention (and money) has been paid to low-intensity conflict, the nation's special operators have seen a lot of action. In nearly every significant U.S. military action over the past 15 years, Special Operations units have been the first to arrive in hostile territory. They started Operation Desert Storm with a daring aerial assault miles behind enemy lines. During the same war, teams moved into Iraq and provided valuable intelligence on enemy activities and conditions. In Panama and Grenada, they captured airfields, military and government buildings, and communication facilities. These highly trained units have become sought-after instructors in the art of unconventional warfare to the world's military forces.

Only a few years ago, most of their missions were attempts to put out fires in the world's hot spots. But more recently, they have embarked on a dizzying variety of humanitarian missions—from Somalia and Rwanda to helping secure the peace in Bosnia. These days, special operators are almost as likely to supervise food and medical aid missions as they are to fire their weapons or blow up bridges. To carry out their missions, they learn to operate with little or no food, to sleep in jungles, mountains, and deserts, and to move through sea, air, and swamp. They leap out of planes at 20,000 feet, swim silently for miles through cold ocean water, and pack more information into their heads in a few months than some college graduates do in years.

Special Operations training is intense and nearly nonstop. While troops in conventional units start their days at 7 or 8 A.M. and go home at 5 P.M., special operators are at their best at night. They are as likely to wake up in a sleeping bag in the Alaska cold, or the Nevada heat, or at a base in Bosnia or Bolivia, as in a comfortable bed back home. Some are away on training or missions for more than seven months each year.

All this training means that these warriors are more expensive to maintain than the conventional soldier or sailor, but it is necessary because so much more is expected of them. They also receive greater freedom. They follow orders, but are encouraged to discuss options and offer a better plan. After all, they operate in small groups with such limited firepower that a poorly conceived mission will invariably lead to failure. Unlike conventional military units which use overwhelming numbers and firepower to vanquish battlefield opponents, special operators rely on stealth, surprise, speed, and above all, good intelligence. When they have all four, special operators can pull off even the most unlikely missions. When they do not, they often end up facing a much larger, better-equipped force.

But as much as the world has changed over the past 35 years, and as much as Special Operations Forces has evolved, the units would still be recognizable to President John F. Kennedy, who was their first great champion. Their mission then was to fight wars against smallish bands of communist insurgents. Kennedy announced, "This is another type of warfare, new in its intensity, ancient in its art . . . war by guerillas, subversives, insurgents, assassins . . . war by ambush, instead of by combat . . . war by infiltration instead of aggression. . . . If freedom is to be saved, we need a whole new kind of strategy, a wholly different kind of force, and therefore a new and wholly different kind of military training." Though the threat has shifted from communist insurgencies and Soviet tanks rolling over the plains of Western Europe to terrorists, nuclear proliferation, and sophisticated drug operators, Kennedy's predictions of the battles of the future remain right on target. "The Quiet Professionals" are ready to fight these battles.

CHAPTER ONE THE NAVY SEALS

Over the years, a number of movies, books, and television shows have attempted to describe Navy SEALs, but none more colorfully than that offered by a former SEAL himself. He described his teammates as "gen-u-wine, shockproof, waterproof, chrome-plated, antimagnetic, barrel-chested, rootin' tootin,' parachutin,' fightin' frogmen, who never eat or sleep, and can breathe underwater and fly."

While quite possibly a stretch of his enthusiasm, history shows Navy SEALs to be an extraordinarily disciplined group of highly trained maritime commandos who see success as their one and only option. SEALs are men of rare courage and valor. Like their predecessors, the frogmen of World War II, Navy SEALs have gone into harm's way under some of the most demanding and hazardous conditions.

In more than 50 years, the values of this elite community have not changed. Navy SEALs place honor, courage, commitment, and integrity above all else. Their complete reliance on teamwork and a sense of dedication is virtually unparalleled. But it's how SEALs do things that has earned them worldwide respect as valiant warriors. The acronym "SEAL" identifies the environments in which they operate (SEa, Air, Land). SEALs are, first and foremost, warriors who come from the sea and return to its silent darkness when their work is done. This distinction alone sets them apart from all other Special Operations Forces. Though one of nature's harshest environments, the water is a safe haven for SEALs. It is where they are most comfortable and confident. It is their ability to operate effectively in small numbers, in and out of the water in a clandestine fashion, that sets Navy SEALs apart from all other fighting forces.

U.S. Navy SEALs of SEAL Team 5 emerge from the water off the coast of California. SEALs were commissioned by President Kennedy in 1962. The SEALs, who derive their name from the elements in which they operate in and from, use the sea for their own strategic and tactical advantage. They are first and foremost a maritime Special Operations Force, whose tactics and techniques are ideally suited to "crisis-action" situations.

The gold Navy SEAL Trident is said to be one of the hardest military insignias to earn. More than 70 percent of all sailors who attempt to achieve it do not measure up for one reason or another. The insignia was adopted in 1971 and is made up of four symbols, which each represent something different. The eagle represents freedom and American ideals and values; the anchor represents the U.S. Navy; the musket represents the right to bear arms and defend those American values; and the trident (a pitchfork-like symbol) denotes the maritime nature of the SEALs.

HISTORY

The Navy SEALs of today enjoy a prestige universally acknowledged. They derive their professionalism and training standards from the legacy of the Scout and Raider (S&R) units and the Naval Combat Demolition Units (NCDUs) of World War II.

Scout and Raider units were initially joint Army and Navy units, but later were composed of all Navy personnel. Scout and Raiders were amphibious reconnaissance units. Their training consisted of six weeks of scout training and six weeks of demolition training. The S&R mission initially focused on special boat operations, long-distance paddling, and infiltration techniques. Their mission further evolved into significant guerrilla operations in China and India, as they operated behind enemy lines. S&R units

distinguished themselves in Europe and the Pacific. The units disbanded after WWII, and many of the individuals and mission skills were absorbed by the Underwater Demolition Teams (UDT).

S&R and NCDU training was an integral part of the U.S. Atlantic Fleet Amphibious Forces training program conducted at Fort Pierce, Florida. Lt. Cmdr. Draper L. Kauffman was hand-selected as the first officer in charge of the NCDU project. Kauffman had a wide range of experience in bomb disposal and demolition work before setting up the vigorous training program at Fort Pierce. His program included the now infamous "Hell Week," which remains a cornerstone event in today's basic SEAL training program. Kauffman remained in the regular Navy after the war and eventually was promoted to the rank of Admiral. SEALs consider Kauffman the "Father of UDT."

NCDU training specifically selected, trained and prepared personnel to remove underwater obstacles. Their simple mission statement:

"To have the responsibility for removing natural and man-made underwater obstacles, which are likely to obstruct landing operations. This mission is performed in close cooperation with other units of the amphibious forces."

NCDU training included the following tasks: handling of explosives, underwater reconnaissance, removal of obstacles, detection of mines and booby traps, seamanship, night vision and observation of coastal silhouettes, use of rubber boats, physical conditioning, long-distance surf swimming with equipment, armed and unarmed combat, stealth and concealment, shallow-water diving, close-order drill, military discipline, and mine sweeping in shallow water. These and other training activities are still part of Navy SEAL team training and qualification programs.

The training course at Fort Pierce normally lasted eight weeks, 10 weeks for some groups (versus 26 weeks in the basic SEAL training course currently). It was a rigorous and concentrated training program, with major emphasis on physical conditioning and drills in removing obstacles through use of hand-placed charges. Instructors considered ability and speed in analyzing and solving demolition problems the most important outcome of the work. The number of trainees dropped during the training program was high—as it is today. Only those fully qualified could continue on to the advanced training and become members of the UDT.

NCDU continued training at Fort Pierce until V-J Day in September 1945. However, the men ordered to duty in the Pacific were assigned to a UDT advanced training base

Students of BUD/S class Number 209 celebrate in the surf zone off on the shores of Coronado, California, moments after their completion of Hell Week during their first phase of BUD/S training. The week, characterized by food and sleep deprivation, is considered to be one of the toughest events on the road to becoming a SEAL. It signifies the end of the first of three phases of training in Coronado.

at Maui, Hawaii, before they were actually assigned to a UDT. Like the UDT men before them, every SEAL operator today must also finish an arduous advanced SEAL Tactical Training course after completing the initial training at Basic Underwater Demolition/SEAL (BUD/S).

At first, NCDUs drew personnel entirely from the ranks of construction battalions (Seabees). Later, they accepted qualified applicants from any branch of the Navy. The first demolition units saw action in Sicily and at Omaha and Utah beaches in Normandy. A Presidential Unit Citation awarded to one of the units described the role of the teams in the landing operations:

"In spite of great handicaps, the demolition crews succeeded initially in blasting five gaps through enemy obstacles for the passage of assault forces to the Normandy shore, and within two days had sapped over 85 percent of the Omaha beach area of the German-placed traps."

When the men returned home from Europe, many were reassigned to duty in the Pacific, where the contemporary Underwater Demolition Teams were born. Each UDT consisted of 8 officers and 120 enlisted men, while each NCDU consisted of 1 officer and 5 enlisted men, or a single boat crew. UDTs conducted operations at Tarawa, Guam, Leyte, Lingayen, Iwo Jima, Okinawa, Balikpapanwi, and throughout the Pacific.

A typical UDT daylight reconnaissance and demolition operation was supported by naval gunfire. Men wearing swim trunks, face masks and swim fins, while carrying knives, watches, compasses, and small slates for recording data, were dropped off boats along a line about 1,500 yards from shore. As they swam toward the beach, they recorded on their slates all natural and constructed obstacles they came across. They swam back to the pick-up line and returned to the main ship, usually a destroyer transport, where personnel studied and evaluated the information. With this data available, another run was made to the beach. This time SEALs brought with them packs of explosives. After placing the explosives and lighting fuses, they once again made their way back to the pick-up site. During these incursions, the UDTs could mark landing areas for the attack boats.

At the end of World War II and throughout the Korean War, the UDTs' numbers decreased to peacetime strengths. The Navy maintained sufficient personnel to satisfy the personnel requirements of four teams. UDT-1 and UDT-12 were established in the Pacific Fleet, while UDT-21 and UDT-22 were established in the Atlantic Fleet. UDT-13 was briefly established in the Pacific near the end of the Korean War and again during the Vietnam War.

SEAL trainee boat crew members hold their Combat Rubber Raiding Craft high above their heads while waiting to enter the surf off Coronado. The 150-pound boat, also known as a Zodiac or CRRC, becomes the crew's constant companion throughout much of training. Each boat crew member must provide his share of the strength it takes to carry the boat, ensuring teamwork for a successful mission.

The Pacific Fleet UDTs were fully involved in Korea. A major amphibious assault occurred at Inchon in September 1950, an action in which the UDTs figured prominently. In addition to preassault duties, the UDTs mapped port facilities, marked natural underwater hazards and areas of reduced depth, cleared mines from rivers and waterways, and conducted commando raids well behind enemy lines. Conducting operations ashore created a new operational dimension for these naval commandos.

As their UDT role expanded tactically, these units performed direct-action demolition missions against supply and transportation lines of communication. They repeated these operations at Wonsan, Iwon, and at the docks of Chinnampo. When faced with Communist China intervention in November 1950, our nation conceived a new use for the evermore versatile UDTs. UDT personnel became guerrilla fighters, generating intelligence and harassing enemy forces deep in their own territory. After Korea, UDTs performed effective combat operations in the Dominican Republic, Cuba, Lebanon, Africa, and other areas throughout the world. Many of their operational exploits remain classified today.

On January 1, 1962, President Kennedy officially signed documentation that led to the establishment of SEAL Teams One and Two in the Pacific and Atlantic fleets respectively. Personnel from the UDTs formed both teams. SEALs trained in guerrilla warfare, counterinsurgency operations, and intelligence collection. The SEAL Teams played a significant role throughout the Vietnam conflict. UDT personnel also conducted numerous beach surveys and tactical hydrographic reconnaissance operations. UDT and SEAL team units and operators were the most highly decorated units assigned to duty in Vietnam.

In 1983, the four remaining UDTs were officially disestablished and reconstructed organizationally into SEAL teams. The SEAL teams subsumed all of the UDT missions, including the mission upon which UDTs were formed—amphibious hydrographic reconnaissance.

SELECTION AND TRAINING

Because success is often determined by the quality of people, Naval Special Warfare (NSW) personnel are carefully selected and trained to perform arduous and inherently treacherous missions, often in circumstances where the reputation of the nation rests on the success of their mission. They remain the most indispensable resource for NSW planning and execution. They do not seek fame or fortune, but rather to be measured by the highest standard of military excellence. Anyone can learn the technical skills required to do the things SEALs do, but few have the personal fortitude

Prospective SEALs train in an exercise that asks them to exchange SCUBA equipment underwater in the Combat Training Tank at Naval Amphibious Base, Coronado. This equipment exchange gives a student an added measure of comfort in the water, and with his equipment, by simulating an emergency situation in which both divers must survive from one man's breathing apparatus.

15

Prospective SEALs train in an exercise called "drownproofing" in the Combat Training Tank at Naval Amphibious Base, Coronado. In this exercise, a sailor's confidence and comfort in the water is built up by letting the sailors prove to themselves that despite being bound at the feet and hands, the men can still survive quite aptly.

to master the mental, physical, and intangible skills needed to be a disciplined warrior. Regardless of their eventual assignment, the first step in that long training process comes at the Naval Special Warfare Center where Basic Underwater Demolition/SEAL (BUD/S) training is conducted. With a dropout rate of approximately 70 percent, success in BUD/S requires an extremely high level of personal commitment. Students encounter obstacles that test their endurance, leadership, and ability to work as a team. SEAL training is so intense that these warriors can never be mass-produced. Because of the dangers inherent in Naval special warfare, prospective SEALs go through what is considered by some to be the toughest military training in the world.

There is an old saying in Texas: It's not the size of the dog in the fight; it's the size of the fight in the dog that counts. When all is said and done, the key to success rests with individual students, who will have to prove many things to many people many times, who will have to control their innermost fears and anxieties, and who must learn who they are and of what they are capable. Most importantly, they must learn their place on the team because at BUD/S there is no "I" in TEAM.

BUD/S training is broken down into three phases. First phase is the basic conditioning phase, which lasts eight weeks. Physical training involves running, swimming, and calisthenics, all of which become increasingly difficult as the weeks progress. The fifth week of training, referred to as "Hell Week," is five and a half days of continuous training with little or no sleep. This week is designed to push the students to their maximum capability, both physically and mentally. The remaining three weeks are spent in hydrographic reconnaissance.

Second phase is the diving phase and is seven weeks in length. Students learn combat SCUBA, both open- and closed-circuit, with emphasis placed on long-distance underwater dives. This training phase prepares the students to be basic combat divers. Third phase involves demolition, reconnaissance, and land warfare training, and is ten weeks in length. This phase concen-

trates on teaching land navigation, small-unit tactics, patrolling techniques, rappelling, and the handling of individual infantry weapons and military explosives. The final four weeks are spent at San Clemente Island, where students apply techniques acquired throughout training in a practical environment.

After graduation, trainees receive three weeks of basic parachuting at Fort Benning, Georgia. They are then assigned to a SEAL or SDV team to complete a six-month probationary period before earning the coveted Naval Special Warfare insignia.

In addition to BUD/S, the Naval Special Warfare Center conducts 11 advanced courses and has six more classes under development to be taught in the near future. These include a two-week course on the MK 15 underwater breathing apparatus (UBA), the most complex diving equipment that Naval Special Warfare utilizes. It is being replaced by the MK 16 UBA, with future courses reflecting the change.

Additional courses conducted by the Naval Special Warfare Center include the following:

- The SEAL Delivery Vehicle (SDV) course is ten weeks long and conducted three times a year. It teaches all the SDV systems and Standard Operating Procedures and is required before students are permitted to dive and operate SDVs.
- The SDV Electronic Maintenance course is eight weeks long and exposes electronic technicians to all the SDV electronic systems, giving them hands-on experience in troubleshooting and repair.
- The two-week Special Operations Technician (SOT) course enables trainees going to NSW commands to diagnose and treat diving-related disorders, using a hyperbaric chamber if necessary.
- The Diving Supervisor course is two weeks long and held four times a year. It is designed for personnel in pay grades E-5 and higher from Joint Special Operations Force commands. Students learn to give diving supervisor briefs and inspections on open-circuit and closed-circuit diving equipment.
- The one-week Diving Maintenance course emphasizes disassembly, reassembly, and maintenance of open circuit and LAR V diving rigs.
- The Maritime Operations (MAROPS) is a three-week course held four times a year. Emphasis is on long-range, over-the-horizon navigation of Combat Rubber Raiding Craft (CRRC) utilizing dead reckoning, compass, and Global Positioning Systems (GPS).
- The Military Free-Fall

Struggling with a problem during a classroom session on navigation, SEAL trainees try to properly plot their course from given waypoints in an attempt to determine time, distance, and ocean current calculations for the operations area. Trainees will go through numerous hours of classroom sessions on topics that range from the physics of diving to land navigation.

First phase SEAL trainees struggle in the surf zone in their Combat Rubber Raiding Craft as they practice repetitive surf zone entries and exits. While these trainees struggle in the surf at this point, they will learn to do this maneuver in a flawless fashion by the end of their training evolution. Potential SEALs whose training happens to be during winter have larger waves to contend with.

(MFF) is a high-risk, three-week course teaching the techniques and safety procedures of free-fall parachuting.

- The Static Line Jump Master course is two weeks long and designed to teach NSW personnel to conduct static line parachute operations.
- The Ram Air Parachute Transition (RAPT) is a one-week course and presently only taught to Explosive Ordnance (EOD) personnel. It emphasizes parachuting with the MT1-XS utilizing a static line.
- The SEAL Weapons System (SWS) course is two weeks and teaches advanced underwater demolition techniques with emphasis on equipment and obstacle loading techniques.
- The Special Warfare Combatant Craft Crewmember (SWCC) Program is a six-week course that teaches the specialized skills required to serve on various Special Operations crafts.

SEAL trainees climb the cargo net on the O-Course (obstacle course) at Coronado. Trainees are timed in their course evolutions and are expected to improve these times as training progresses. Many obstacles not only test physical strength and agility, but mental strength and determination. Toward the end of the training cycle at Coronado, most SEAL trainees look forward to the O-Course, a far different emotion from what they felt the first few times they encountered it.

Established in 1993, it created a new enlisted classification for sailors who drive the various boats essential to the SEALs' highly sensitive and often hazardous operations.

For Navy SEALs, training is never complete. Whether assigned to a SEAL team, SDV team, or a Special Boat squadron, SEALs are constantly refining their unique skills and adopting new ways of operating that will better prepare them for future missions.

ORGANIZATION

Today, the major operational components of Naval Special Warfare Command include Naval Special Warfare Group One and Special Boat Squadron One in Coronado, California, and Naval Special Warfare Group Two and Special Boat Squadron Two in Little Creek, Virginia. Other major component commands are Naval Special Warfare Development Group in Dam Neck, Virginia, and Naval Special Warfare Center in Coronado, California.

Since the close of the Vietnam conflict, ever-changing world situations have resulted in increased operational tasks. NSW units are homeported in Panama, Germany, Puerto Rico, Guam, Spain, and a unit soon to be established in Bahrain. Post-Vietnam operations where Naval Special Warfare forces have distinguished themselves include Urgent Fury (Grenada 1983); Earnest Will (Persian Gulf, 1987–1990); Just Cause

(Panama, 1989–1990); and Desert Shield/Desert Storm (Middle East, 1990–1991). More recently, SEALs have conducted missions in Somalia, Bosnia, Haiti, and Liberia.

The organization and people of Naval Special Warfare represent two separate professional communities, the individual SEALs and Special Boat crews. Each are distinctively different, yet complementary in every respect. Each prepares separately but they train together to conduct short-notice, small-unit operations at night. From over the horizon, they infiltrate from sea, air, or land in adverse weather.

Within NSW, Special Boat squadrons are teamed with SEALs to provide mutual support. Their principal responsibility is to provide the SEAL teams with dedicated mobility however, they have broader capabilities to support fleet and joint task force commanders in shallow-water areas, where larger ships cannot go. The NSW Special Boat Squadrons maintain a complete inventory of combatant craft and ships that complement the Navy's overall mission. Their primary focus remains the clandestine infiltration and extraction of SEALs or other Special Operations Forces (SOF).

Just as the SEALs have a menu of weapons from which to select for each mission, the Special Boat squadrons have a complete menu of inflatable boats, combatant craft, and ships. They range from rigid-hull inflatable boats (RHIBs) to 170-foot Patrol

Navy SEAL student boat crews perform log physical training, also known as log PT. Students run and exercise with these logs, running races between boat crews, doing sit ups and other calisthenics. The logs instill teamwork and determination.

Doing their best to raise a 300-pound log above their heads, Navy SEAL student boat crews perform log PT. Crews not performing up to par, according to the instructors, will be given a heavier log said to weigh approximately 400 pounds.

Coastal (PC) class ships, and include vessels designed primarily for riverine and near-shore operations. NSW special boats are not slated for any definitive single mission. Experience has demonstrated that craft will be mixed and matched to meet operational situations, and that craft primarily designed for high-speed ocean transit may also conduct riverine operations. NSW has developed an unsurpassed inventory of combatant craft and ships, each inherently capable of conducting multiple missions. Special Boat personnel, experts in small-boat operations, are also trained to handle enemy or civilian boats commandeered during operations throughout the world.

Special Boat crews are carefully selected through records reviews. Once assigned to a particular combatant craft or ship, they train extensively in craft and weapons tactics, techniques, and procedures. This in-depth training allows them to qualify for special Navy classifications, a five-year continuous command assignment, and sequential or future Special Boat assignments. No military organization in the world spends more time or is better qualified at operating combatant craft and small submersibles, conducting bubble-free diving and combat swimming or clandestinely infiltrating hostile shorelines. The mobility of NSW forces and the wide variety of delivery methods offer unparalleled ability to rapidly and unobtrusively place small groups of skilled and disciplined naval commandos into areas of national interest.

NSW's unique and specialized SEAL Delivery Vehicle (SDV) teams are trained and organized to operate the nation's inventory of combatant submersibles, frequently called "mini-submarines." SDV teams can respond to global tasking on short notice. When employed with fleet nuclear submarines equipped with dry deck shelters, SDVs offer the most clandestine means of infiltration of any military force. Without ever breaking the surface of the water, the SDV can deliver SEALs or explosives, lay limpet mines, or conduct close-in intelligence collection in the enemy's presence. This maritime-military capability is unsurpassed in the world.

SEALs and Special Boats offer a focused global response to hostile situations not requiring large conventional forces; yet they can easily work in support of a large force. Their tactical strengths are flexibility, mobility, stealth, firepower, and individual discipline, nerve, and courage.

All who earn and wear the Trident insignia of the SEALs belong to the most highly trained and motivated fighting force in the world. The SEAL Team remains the only organization in the U.S. military in which individuals can volunteer to join or volunteer to be dropped from the program. Naval Special Warfare personnel are SEAL officers and enlisted operators who represent one of the four major Navy warfare specialties (Surface, Subsurface, Air, and Naval Special Warfare).

EQUIPMENT

The need to adapt to a quickly changing world makes essential the continuous review of training, policy, doctrine, and the tools SEALs use to accomplish their missions. NSW must be able to support fleet and joint task force commanders across the spectrum of peacetime and wartime conflict. It remains a comprehensive challenge and responsibility to ensure that NSW personnel are trained and equipped with the finest and most modern equipment in the world.

NSW does not need capability-enhancing equipment in large quantities, but its equipment must be designed to withstand the rigors of hostile operating environments. SEAL missions range from high-altitude parachuting to long-duration diving operations. They involve clandestine operations from rubber raiding craft and high-speed combatant craft, land-patrolling skills and combat swimming or shallow-water diving in dark, cold or murky waters using sophisticated breathing-gas mixtures and protective suits. Equipment design and construction costs are often high because of small inventory quantities; however, because NSW forces cannot fail when they are asked to execute, ensuring proper design and construction remains a cost-effective approach in the overall budget.

PATROL COASTAL CLASS SHIPS

The 13 Patrol Coastal class ships are assigned to the Special Boat Squadrons One and Two, based at San Diego, California, and Norfolk, Virginia, respectively. The following units make up the Patrol Coastal class: Cyclone (PC-1); Tempest (PC-2); Hurricane (PC-3); Monsoon (PC-4); Typhoon (PC-5); Sirocco (PC-6); Squall (PC-7); Zephyr (PC-8); Chinook (PC-9); Firebolt (PC-10); Whirlwind (PC-11); Thunderbolt (PC-12); and Shamal (PC-13).

The PCs have a primary mission of coastal patrol and interdiction, with a secondary mission of Naval Special Warfare support. Primary employment missions include forward presence, monitoring and detection operations, escort operations, noncombatant evacuation, and foreign internal defense. The PC class operates in low-intensity conflict environments. Naval Special Warfare operational missions include long-range SEAL insertion and extraction, tactical swimmer operations, intelligence collection, operational deception, and coastal and riverine support.

SPECIAL OPERATIONS CRAFT

The MARK V Special Operations Craft is the newest, most versatile, high-performance combatant craft introduced into the Naval Special Warfare Special Boat squadron inventory to enhance maritime special operations capabilities. The mission of the MARK V is to support maritime medium-range insertion and extraction of Special Operations Forces, primarily SEAL combat swimmers, in low- to medium-threat environments. It is also designated to support limited coastal reconnaissance and surveillance.

MARK Vs are organized into detachments, which comprise two craft, crews, and a deployment support package mounted on cargo transporters. The detachment can be delivered in-theater rapidly by two C-5 aircraft, by well- or flight-deck equipped surface vessel or, if appropriate, on their own ship's power. The detachment will be deployable within 48 hours of notification and ready for operations within 24 hours of arrival at a forward operating base. They can operate from shoreline facilities, from well-deck equipped ships or from ships with appropriate crane and deck space capabilities.

The MARK Vs are a product of a streamlined acquisition effort managed by the U.S. Special Operations

SEAL trainees paddle ashore in their Combat Rubber Raiding Craft as they practice repetitive surf zone entries and exits. They are learning valuable lessons on how to work as a team to enter and exit the surf area quickly.

BUD/S students line up in the murky water of the Demolition Pit, a large pit with a set of ropes strung from one end to the other. Here, students who have tried to cross the ropes that lie approximately 10 feet above the water, wade shoulder deep and shiver with cold as they watch their counterparts attempt the same task on the last day of Hell Week.

A BUD/S student in his boat crew strains to hold up their Combat Rubber Raiding Craft (CRRC), after not having the opportunity to empty all of the sea water out of the boat after coming ashore. The Zodiac, as it is also known, weighs 150 pounds and can easily become twice that if a crew does not properly empty the water upon coming ashore. A UDT/SEAL instructor will drive this point home by having that crew hold their boat over their head for a longer period of time.

A sailor responds to a Master Chief UDT/SEAL instructor as the student and others in his class are asked if they are ready to be secured at the end of Hell Week. The end of Hell Week marks a milestone in a trainee's attempt to become a SEAL. After a week of food and sleep deprivation, most trainees spend the following day eating and sleeping, before beginning the second phase of training.

Coxswains line up in front of their boat crews and respond with loud yells during the last moments of Hell Week. The end of Hell Week is a time most BUD/S students hope they'll see. Considered to be one of the defining moments of SEAL training, it is a point where many drop out due to the emotional and physical strain.

Command's Special Operations Acquisition Executive. From the time the contract was awarded to the time NSW took possession of the first two craft was only 18 months.

RIVER PATROL BOAT

The River Patrol Boat (PBR) is designed for high-speed riverine patrol operations in contested areas of operations, and insertion and extraction of SEAL team elements. More than 500 units were built when first introduced in the Vietnam conflict in 1966, although the current inventory is 24 craft. They can be transported in C-5 aircraft on skids. The PBR is heavily armed and vital crew areas are protected with ceramic armor. The weapons loadout on this craft includes both single and twin .50 caliber machine gun mounts, 40-mm grenade launchers, and various small arms.

The hull is reinforced fiberglass, with two Jacuzzi-type water jet pumps for propulsion, making it possible for the unit to operate in shallow, debris-filled water. The craft is highly maneuverable and can turn 180 degrees and reverse course within the distance of its own length while operating at full power. Engine noise silencing techniques have been incorporated into the design and improved over the years. The combination of relatively quiet operation and its onboard surface search radar system make this unit an excellent all-weather picket, as well as a shallow-water patrol and interdiction craft.

Lined up along the beach, boat crews hold their CRRCs above their heads and wait for the next command from the UDT/SEAL instructors. BUD/S students will often find themselves in formations such as this, and they are often asked to hold it longer if everything is not done right.

RIGID HULL INFLATABLE BOAT

The Rigid Hull Inflatable Boat (RHIB) is a high-speed, high-buoyancy, extreme-weather craft with the primary mission of insertion and extraction of SEAL tactical elements from enemy-occupied beaches. It is constructed of glass-reinforced plastic with an inflatable tube gunwale made of a new hypalon neoprene and nylon-reinforced fabric. There are two types of RHIBs currently in the inventory: a 24-foot RHIB and a 30-foot RHIB. The RHIB has demonstrated the ability to operate in light-loaded condition in sea state six and winds of 45 knots. For other than heavy weather coxswain training, operations are limited to sea state five and winds of 34 knots or less. The RHIB carries a crew of three and a SEAL element. A 10-meter RHIB is currently in acquisition to provide for a SEAL squad delivery capability.

MINI-ARMORED TROOP CARRIER

The Mini-Armored Troop Carrier (MATC) is a 36-foot, all-aluminum hull craft designed for high-speed patrol, interdiction, and combat assault missions in rivers, harbors, and protected coastal areas. The MATC has a large well area for transporting combat-equipped troops, carrying cargo, or for gunnery personnel operating the seven organic weapon stations. Its propulsion system is similar to that of the MK II PBR, with an internal jet pump that moves the water on the same principle as the air-breathing jet engine. This type of propulsion is especially appropriate for beaching operations. A hydraulic bow ramp is designed to aid the insertion and extraction of troops and equipment.

The craft has a low silhouette, which makes it difficult to detect in all speed ranges. The unit is extremely quiet, particularly at idle speeds. An onboard high resolution radar and multiple communications suite provides good all-weather surveillance and command and control presence for interdiction and antismuggler operations. The overhead canopy can be removed or stowed below. Crew size is normally four but can be modified depending on the mission and its duration.

COMBAT RUBBER RAIDING CRAFT

The Combat Rubber Raiding Craft are used for clandestine surface insertion and extraction of lightly armed amphibious forces. They are employed to land and recover U.S. Marine Corps reconnaissance squads and SEALs from over-the-horizon. The CRRC is capable of surf passages. It may be launched by air (rubber duck/helo-cast), by landing craft utility or landing craft medium (mike boats). It may also be deck-launched from submarines. It has a low visual electronic signature and is capable of being cached by its crew once ashore. It uses 35–55 horsepower engines.

A SEAL trainee walks through the Cleveland National Forest in California performing a land navigation exercise. Carrying a full 60-pound pack, trainees will find their way through three to four kilometers of mountainous, high-elevation terrain, using only a compass and a map. Their final exam for this week-long portion of training consists of a course in which trainees must correctly find different checkpoints, where they each are given a heading for the next successive point. The course can take some trainees upwards of five hours, but most will finish in four. The longer the time, the better the chance that they will be sent out to do it all over again.

A view of the Mark V Special Operations Craft (SOC) as it speeds across the open ocean at 50 knots. The high-performance craft is designed to carry a crew of 16 SEALs or other Special Operations Forces for medium-range insertion or extraction. It has a crew of five, a range in excess of 600 nautical miles, and is sized to be transported by air aboard a C-5 aircraft.

SEAL DELIVERY VEHICLE AND DRY DECK SHELTER

The SEAL Delivery Vehicle (SDV) combatant submersible and the Dry Deck Shelter (DDS) deep-dive system operate in conjunction with fleet nuclear submarines; and the MK V Special Operations Craft and Patrol Coastal class ships also provide unique and organic capabilities for SEAL infiltration from the sea. The SDV MK VIII is a "wet" submersible, designed to carry combat swimmers and their cargo in fully flooded compartments. Submerged operators and passengers are sustained by the individually worn underwater breathing apparatus. Operational scenarios for the vehicle include underwater mapping and terrain exploration, location and recovery of lost or downed objects, and reconnaissance missions.

A SEAL exits a SEAL Delivery Vehicle (SDV) in the waters off Hawaii. The SDV is deployed from a submarine and is designed to carry combat swimmers and their cargo in fully flooded compartments. Submerged operators and passengers are sustained by their individually worn SCUBA gear. This vehicle allows SEALs' to be deployed in a clandestine fashion, arrive at their target undetected, and return to the submarine over the span of several hours. It is the SEALs ability to operate so effectively underwater that makes them a unique asset to Special Operations missions. *U.S. Navy Photo*

A crew member aboard a Mark V Special Operations Craft uses hand signals to direct the approach of SEAL teams in Combat Rubber Raiding Crafts (CRRC). The CRRCs will drive right up onto the slanted deck of the moving Mark V.

The vehicle is propelled by an all-electric propulsion subsystem powered by rechargeable silver-zinc batteries. Buoyancy and pitch attitude are controlled by a ballast and trim system, and control in both the horizontal and vertical planes is provided through a manual control stick to the rudder, elevator, and bow planes. A computerized Doppler navigation sonar displays speed, distance, heading, altitude, and other piloting functions. Instruments and other electronics units are housed in dry, watertight canisters. The special modular construction provides easy removal for maintenance.

The dry deck shelter (DDS) allows submarines to participate in special operations involving the SDV. The DDS launches and recovers the SDV while the host ship is submerged. The DDS is installed on the host ship immediately

A trainee strains to complete one of the countless number of pull-ups he will do throughout his evolution on his way to becoming a SEAL. Seventy percent of the trainees who start the BUD/S program never make it, and return to the fleet.

before the SDV mission and is removed when the mission is completed. The host ship can carry one DDS or two DDSs mounted side by side. The installation of the DDS does not affect the performance of the host ship appreciably. The few permanent modifications made to the ship do not degrade ship performance after the DDS has been removed.

The DDS consists of three pressure modules constructed as one integral unit: a hangar in which the SDV and

Doing an exercise called "dips," a BUD/S student strains to push himself back upright and lock his arms straight. Physical training and conditioning are stressed throughout the Special Operations community as soldiers and sailors are often asked to take themselves to their limits and beyond.

Due to its overall design, the Mark V Special Operations Craft (SOC) is difficult to detect on radar. Although it wasn't built from the ground up as a stealth boat, it has many features that make it less detectable than other boats similar in size.

other system equipment are stowed, a transfer trunk to allow passage between the modules and the host ship, and a hyperbaric chamber for decompression and recompression treatment of divers. Penetrations between DDS modules are made through the attachment rings, which have faces to accommodate the penetrations. The DDS provides a working environment at one atmosphere for the mission team during transit and has structural integrity to test the depth of the host ship. The DDS can be provided with a hangar door that opens to starboard or to port.

ADVANCED SEAL DELIVERY SYSTEM

The ability to conduct clandestine insertion and extraction of SEAL squads into high-threat environments is essential to Naval Special Warfare. The Advanced SEAL Delivery System (ASDS) will do just that. Transportable by C-5 aircraft, the ASDS is a manned, dry interior, combatant submersible with the requisite range endurance, speed, payload, and other capabilities for conducting a full range of hostile operations. Detailed design of the vehicle was completed in fiscal year 1994 with three submersibles funded and three more planned in 1998–2003. The host platform for this battery-powered craft is a fast-attack submarine or landing ship dock.

The advantage of the ASDS is that, unlike the MK VIII, which exposes SEALs to extremely cold water for long offshore transits, the ASDS will keep SEALs warm and dry until the start of an operation. Additionally, with the

U.S. Navy SEALs rise from the water and cover their points of fire as they do a quick area recon of the area where they've surfaced. To protect themselves and ensure a quick response if fired upon, SEALs will position themselves back to back to afford to them a 360-degree view. SEALs are traditionally some of the first battle forces on scene, to clear the way for other follow-on forces. They become the eyes and ears for the rest of the fleet.

Aboard a CRRC with SEALs from SEAL Team 3. They are getting ready to board a moving Mark V boat cruising just ahead.

Teams of SEAL trainees climb ropes as instructors make this day CEs event a competition. The winner of each evolution is allowed to go to chow, while the losing teams must stay and compete against each other. In BUD/S, winning and being the best has its advantages, and instructors reward that characteristic.

A fully loaded SEAL moves through the woods toward the next checkpoint. With their navigation skills, SEALs can cover many miles of rugged terrain and still arrive precisely at their objectives.

ASDS, SEALs will be able to loiter for a longer period of time and be able to start from farther out at sea.

DESERT PATROL / LIGHT STRIKE VEHICLE

The Desert Patrol/Light Strike Vehicle (DPV) is a modified Chenoweth off-road, 2x4 racing vehicle, with the addition of a third seat for a gunner and additional mounts for weapon systems to enhance their survivability. The DPV was designed to operate anywhere a four-wheel drive vehicle can, with additional speed and maneuverability. It can perform numerous combat roles including, but not limited to, a Special

Operations delivery vehicle, command and control vehicle, weapons platform, rear area combat operation vehicle, reconnaissance vehicle, forward observation and lasing team, military police vehicle, and artillery forward observer vehicle

The DPVs came into the public eye through their use in Operation Desert Storm. They assisted the SEALs in helping to liberate the U.S. Embassy in Kuwait City and in providing security for the U.S. ambassador upon his return. They were also one of the main modes of land travel by SEAL teams due to their speed, maneuverability, and versatility in the sand.

The Heckler and Koch 9mm MP-5A5 Sub-machine gun, the weapon of choice for SEALs operating from a water environment. SEALs use this weapon when anticipating close quarter battle conditions. Like most things the SEALs use, it withstands exposure to water extremely well.

Navy SEAL basics are the diving mask, fins, attack board, MP-5, and the SCUBA gear of choice, the LAR V Draeger. The Draeger allows the diver to rebreathe his expended air and thus not release air bubbles to the surface that might alert the enemy to his presence.

Navy SEAL sniper rifle is Model 700 Remington .300 Winchester Magnum. With a 10X Leupold day-scope, it is one of three sniper rifles used by the SEALs. The others are the M-14 with a Sniper kit and a McMillien 50 caliber SASR bolt action rifle.

A Motorola LST-5C satellite radio connected to a field tactical satellite antenna provides for secure communications and voice data links with other forces.

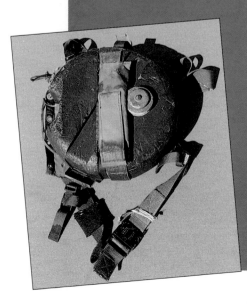

Standard equipment for the SEAL combat swimmer, the neutrally buoyant limpet mine is a high explosive used for disabling and destroying surface vessels. This device is attached to the vessel's hull underwater and set to go off at a precise time after the combat swimmer clears the area.

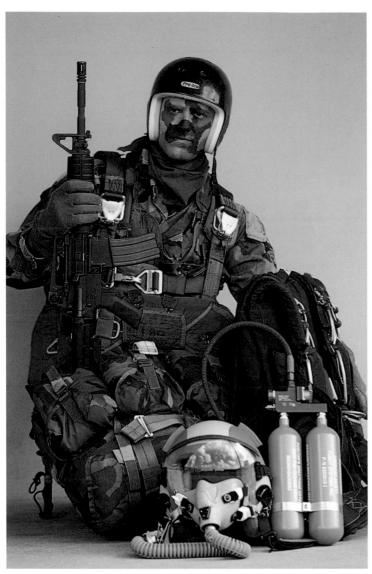

Navy SEAL high altitude parachute equipment, consisting of a helmet, oxygen tanks, mask, and MT-1X parachute. Jump training for SEALs and all other Special Operations Forces is one of the few centralized schools. Static line training is done at Fort Benning, Georgia, while all other initial jump training in done in Yuma, Arizona.

MOBILE COMMUNICATIONS TEAM

The Mobile Communications Team is an operational component of the communications-electronics departments of the Naval Special Warfare Groups based in Coronado, California, and Little Creek, Virginia. They are responsible for providing operational communications support to SEAL teams, SEAL Delivery Vehicle teams, and Special Boat squadrons for deployed fleet and joint units; organizing, training, and integrating new equipment and developing tactics to provide the highest quality Naval Special Warfare communications operations and support; and preparing, implementing, and reviewing communications plans in coordination with higher authority, Naval Special Warfare Command components, and other fleet and joint units.

DIVE GEAR

U.S. Navy SEALs have three life-support systems available for the conduct of Naval Special Warfare operations: open-cir-

cuit compressed air, closed-circuit (100 percent oxygen) LAR V Draeger UBA, and closed-circuit (mixed gas) MK 15 UBA.

In the open-circuit system, air is breathed from a supply tank and exhausted directly into the surrounding water. The supply tank(s) can be worn on the diver (SCUBA), or the diver may breathe from SDV air tanks, if in an SDV. SDV personnel may use SDV-supplied air for long offshore transits and switch to a closed-circuit system in danger areas. Open-circuit systems are limited in duration by the capacity of the air supply, depth, dive work rate, and water temperature. Long-duration deep dives may require diver decompression.

The LAR V Draeger is a self-contained closed-circuit, 100 percent oxygen, underwater breathing apparatus, designed for clandestine operations in shallow water. The LAR V is worn on the diver's chest. With this closed-circuit system, the diver breathes 100 percent oxygen, and exhaled breath is recirculated in the diving apparatus. The diver's exhaled breath passes through a chemical filter that removes carbon dioxide, replenishing the oxygen consumed. Depth, water temperature, and oxygen consumption rate all affect the duration of the LAR V Draeger.

The MK 15 is a self-contained, closed-circuit, mixed-gas, underwater breathing apparatus. The breathing gas is completely retained within the apparatus except during ascent, when excess pressure is vented. In the MK 15, oxygen is mixed and diluted with a gas (normally air) to maintain a preset partial pressure of oxygen (PPO2) level. The constantly preset PPO2 level increases the depth and duration capability as compared to a 100 percent oxygen system. The duration of the MK 15 is limited by the carbon dioxide scrubber canister. Long-duration deep dives may require diver decompression.

MISSIONS

The term "Navy SEALs" conjures images of danger, intrigue, and excitement, and strikes a vision of the consummate naval commando. Generally, they conduct operations such as reconnaissance, intelligence collection, and a variety of swift and often violent direct-action sabotage raids or demolition missions against personnel or targets in hostile or restricted environments. SEAL operations, as with most Special Operations missions, are not for the faint of heart. SEALs and their supporting special boats, craft, and ships offer a unique combination of clandestine operations, intense attack, and surgical application of force, and they use the sea in a manner to which no enemy can compare.

SEALs are the eyes and ears of the fleet. They are almost always the first to enter a hostile area. Intelligence collection, raids and ambushes, combat search and rescue, training of foreign military forces, and counterterror-

Over the years SEALs missions have grown to encompass many land warfare missions. Although the most common images of SEALs are associated with water operations, SEALs also distinguished themselves during Vietnam as a highly mobile and highly capable ground combat force. The weapon used by many SEALs when on land is a CAR-15, a short version of the M-16 rifle.

Members of SEAL Team 5 spread out and take defensive positions to secure their area after fast roping down from two Sikorsky SH-60 Seahawk helicopters. The SEALs were the first to use this fast roping technique in a combat environment in Grenada.

Two groups of men from SEAL Team 5 perform SPIE rig training with the help of two Sikorsky SH-60 Seahawk helicopters. This effective means of insertion and extraction allows a team to be dropped in and "plucked" out of a pinpoint area.

Just back from an extended swim, BUD/S students shiver from the cold as an instructor gives them directions for their next task. Always kept busy, SEAL trainees are rarely given much time to rest. Mental and physical tasks keep them challenged up to their limits.

ism and counternarcotics operations are all integral parts of the NSW mission. SEAL elements are compact in size, heavily armed, and highly maneuverable. A key element in their utilization is their ability to conduct missions against targets larger forces cannot approach undetected.

Naval Special Warfare SEAL teams and Special Boat squadrons ultimately carry out the tactical objectives of the Naval Special Warfare Command, which is the Navy component to the U.S. Special Operations Command (SOC). SEALs are also assigned to the theater commanders, and charged with missions of vast international scope. SEALs are a dedicated combat force capable of being projected globally the instant theater commanders need them. They remain, first and foremost, tactical units in service to the Fleet Commander. They routinely deploy with Amphibious Forces and Carrier Battle Groups to provide a variety of ever increasing missions in support of naval and joint commanders in all theaters.

Naval Special Warfare operations are inherently joint in nature. They frequently rely heavily on Marines or other military branch units for insertion, extraction, and other combat support. On a day-to-day basis, NSW forces are assigned under the operational control of the Commander-in-Chief, U.S. Special Operations Command, headquartered in Tampa, Florida.

When supported by a host ship or submarine, SEALs launch most operations from their own raiding craft or specialized combatant submersible vehicles. SEALs who require tactical medium- or long-range transits for infiltration are launched from combatant surface craft and ships organic to the Special Boat squadrons. Many operations are also launched from nuclear submarines, various naval and non-naval ships, and from the air in helicopters or fixed-wing air-

A SEAL team leader signals up to the helicopter that his team is in place and secured to the SPIE (Special Purpose Insertion and Extraction) rigging rope. Upon seeing this hand signal, the pilot will slowly lift the team and fly them to their insertion point.

A sniper from SEAL Team 5 in the brush with his weapon, a Remington .300 caliber Winchester Magnum Long Range Sniper Rifle. SEAL snipers attend a four-week training class to learn the discreet, surgical application of deadly force on targets that range from enemy personnel to military equipment.

Dragging his parachute behind him, a SEAL swims toward a recovery boat after parachuting into the waters off the coast of California during a training mission. During an actual mission, the parachute would probably not be recovered.

craft. The majority of NSW operations originate from sea-based platforms, since 144 of the 170 sovereign nations of the world are directly accessible from the sea or river systems. Approximately half of the world's industry and population is located within one mile of an ocean or navigable waterway.

Globally oriented and suited to operate independently or as part of a joint or naval expeditionary force, NSW task-organized detachments are configured to accomplish flexible and effective response actions. With the detachments of SEALs, combatant craft, coastal patrol ships, combatant submersibles, and command, control, and communications give Joint Task Force Commanders a variety of forward basing options. NSW forces deploy as organic elements and require little support in a nonprotracted environment. They can be remotely based, operate from existing bases or be based afloat with naval combatants, submarines, floating barges, or almost any vessel of opportunity. At any given moment, one-quarter to one-third of all of the nation's SEALs and Special Boats are forward deployed in support of the Department of Defense's five war-fighting regional commanders. Others remain in training throughout the country and on immediate standby for rapid air or sea deployment in time of crisis. All are prepared to employ as a maritime global strike force at a moment's notice, or as part of a Special Operations surge-force package to augment existing theater-based forces.

Members of SEAL Team 5 parachute into the water using an MT-1B parachute. Such an insertion allows for a Team and their CRRC to drop into a specified location anywhere within a matter of hours.

Although rarely seen and never voluntarily advertised, these NSW quiet professionals deploy to nearly every hot spot in the world. They deploy ashore with allied counterparts or with other U.S. forces, or aboard Navy aircraft carriers, amphibious assault ships, and other military platforms. SEALs and Special Boat personnel are geographically oriented to deal with the terrain and environmental conditions of their intended operational areas. They routinely train in desert, jungle, mountain, Arctic, and urban warfare. Frequently called the "Warriors of the Night," SEALs use the night as a shield and the water and weather as allies. They also retain the skills essential to effectively operate in peacetime or in less-than-sophisticated operational environments.

The traditional NSW role in coalition building through exercises and Foreign Internal Defense (FID) efforts is receiving increased emphasis. Furthermore, because they have often been employed during operations other than war, NSW forces routinely work with U.S. agencies outside of the Department of Defense. Many receive training in foreign languages and regional customs. Because of their ties to the various services, allies and other governmental agencies, interoperability has long been a goal of Naval Special Warfare. NSW personnel having direct interaction with foreign counterparts significantly impact country-to-country relationships, and often are the only U.S. personnel serving as "grass-roots" ambassadors representing the values of our nation. This kind of nation-to-nation contact has a lasting impact when many of these junior counterparts progress to positions as senior military officers or political or business leaders.

RIGHT

Strapping on an MT-1B parachute rig for an over-water jump, a SEAL gets ready to board a C-130 aircraft for a daylight, over-water insertion. The C-130 will deploy the SEALs and a CRRC (known as a "rubber duck" when used in this way) to a predetermined point over the sea.

MIDDLE

SEAL Team 5 members gather their gear for a ride out to the jump site. The rear cargo ramp of the C-130 opens in flight, providing a clear area for the SEALs and their gear to exit the aircraft.

LOWER RIGHT

Six members of SEAL Team 3 jump from the C-130 one after the other. The SEALs must exit the aircraft quickly after the person before them to keep the team together. Any hesitation increases the chance of being separated from the rest of the team and having a longer swim.

BELOW

Waiting for instructions for their next waterborne task, BUD/S students listen attentively to a UDT/SEAL instructor during their fourth week of training. Nearly 70 percent of those who began training have dropped out by now.

NSW forces employ for tactical intelligence collection or surgical raids. NSW offers economy of scale and is used as a force multiplier when training or advising allied forces. By virtue of their small, flexible nature and surgical strike capability, NSW forces are ideally suited for contribution at all levels of conflict. They work best from the water, but are trained and prepared to excel on land as well. SEALs operate out of all proportion to their number in order to limit armed encounters. When military commanders must apply force incrementally and precisely, NSW forces provide necessary and viable options. Their tactics and techniques are ideally suited to "crisis-action" situations. They are most effective when they carry out missions and leave undetected. When required, however, they can bring substantial fire power to bear on selective targets. Special weapons exist to damage or destroy a single individual or a single ship the size of an aircraft carrier.

NSW Command has established aggressive training programs designed to support the operational needs and requirements of fleet and joint force commanders. SEALs and Special Boat Squadrons routinely train and deploy with the naval surface force, naval air force and naval submarine force. During preparation for deployment overseas and actual deployments, NSW personnel operate as a integrated team in war-fighting elements called NSW task groups or units. They are commanded by senior SEAL officers, who function as Special Operations advisors, planners, and command and control agents for numbered fleet commanders or Joint Special Operations Task Force commanders afloat or ashore. NSW forces embarked with Navy shipboard commanders are fully integrated into the mission of the fleet and its contingency plans. They fulfill a variety of doctrinal missions, such as reconnaissance and surveillance (in and out of the water), combat search and rescue, sniper missions, aircraft laser-bomb target designating, ship limpet-mine attacks, and hostile under-way ship assaults or takedowns.

As the Navy's focus shifts more toward coastal areas, and the fleet is shaped for expanded joint operations and operations forward from the sea, new roles are being discovered every day for NSW support of the fleet. NSW remains a unique part of the navy family. They are currently the only designated U.S. Special Operations Force unit, under the command of U.S. Special Operations Command, having a mission within its parent service.

Drawing upon the proud traditions of the Underwater Demolition Teams and the Scouts and Raiders of World War II, the SEALs and Special Boats were baptized in the rivers and jungles of Vietnam, and are now located at every corner of the earth. Naval Special Warfare forces stand ready as on-call, national-level assets. They train as the force of choice in crisis situations. They can deploy on short notice and be prepared to conduct operations immediately upon arrival in the action area. Some NSW units are staged for deployment within 24 hours time. Others deploy within 48 hours, and none will require longer than 72 hours. There is no comparable military force anywhere in the world.

Because the future is difficult to forecast under the best of circumstances, NSW missions continues to require stealth and surprise in an environment where active and passive detection capabilities continue to improve. Known and potential technologies must continue to be used and explored for NSW to fully support national policy objectives.

Packing a 50 caliber machine gun, a 40-mm grenade launcher facing forward, and a 7.62-mm machine gun covering the rear, the DPV carries quite a bit of firepower for a vehicle its size. Its roof racks carry portable anti-aircraft or antitank missiles as well.

Based on the design of an off-road racing vehicle, the Desert Patrol Vehicle (DPV) carries a crew of three, a driver, a commander, and a gunner. Demonstrated here by members of SEAL Team 3, the DPV first came into the public eye during its use in Operation Desert Storm.

DPVs assisted SEALs in liberating the U.S. Embassy in Kuwait City and provided security for the U.S. ambassador upon his return. They were one of the main modes of land travel by SEALs in the Gulf War due to their speed, maneuverability, and versatility in the sand. The vehicle employs the use of six different weapons systems and can reach speeds in excess of 60 miles per hour.

CHAPTER TWO

THE ARMY RANGERS

Of all of America's Army Special Operations Forces, the U.S. Army Rangers have the longest history and pack the most firepower when committed to combat. Their lineage is the basis for other Special Operations Forces within the Army; their techniques and tactics have been tested in the fires of combat around the world, as well as here in the United States. Ranger tactics evolved from the simple ambushes of the Revolutionary War–era Rangers to the sophisticated, airfield-seizure missions of the present-day 75th Ranger Regiment.

Rangers have seen combat in every major conflict in which the United States has participated. They are considered the finest light-infantry force in the world by friend and foe alike. Their tenacity in battle has earned them streamers and awards from a grateful nation. This intense desire to win has manifested itself through the dedication and esprit de corps of the Ranger Regiment. It is poignantly stated in the fifth stanza of the Ranger Creed:

"Energetically will I meet the enemies of my country. I shall defeat them on the field of battle for I am better trained and will fight with all my might. Surrender is not a Ranger word. I will never leave a fallen comrade to fall into the hands of the enemy and under no circumstances will I ever embarrass my country."

HISTORY
REVOLUTIONARY AND CIVIL WARS

The force, whose members wear a distinctive black beret and a "Ranger" scroll, traces its ancestry back to 1756 when Maj. Robert Rogers recruited nine companies of American colonists to fight for the British during the French and Indian War. Rogers

Rangers advance through a trench and bunker system constructed at Fort Lewis during a 12-day battalion movement and evaluation exercise. To maintain a high level of readiness, Rangers are constantly working on their skills. Each battalion can deploy anywhere in the world in 18 hours or less.

Members of a Ranger mortar section fire a round downrange during a live-fire exercise at Fort Lewis, Washington. Mortar units employ the use of a scout, or forward observer (FO) to assist them in range calculations because their intended target is beyond their line of sight.

The FO, from an elevated observation point, will relay to the mortars team his position and distance to the target. The team will triangulate their location, the FO's location, and compute the target's estimated distance, and commence firing. The FO will then be able to indicate to the mortar team any adjustments in range, distance to target, or whether further firepower is needed.

capitalized on the techniques and methods of operation inherent to the American frontiersman and required for survival in the wilds. He incorporated them into a doctrine and philosophy that current Rangers draw on, even today.

Contributing further to the story of the Ranger were the Americans who fought in the Revolutionary War and the Civil War. Men such as Daniel Morgan, creator of Morgan's Riflemen, and Francis Marion, the Swamp Fox, both woodsmen and fighters, worked to make the most of the natural abilities of the fron-

tiersmen they led. They were followed, during the Civil War, by John S. Mosby, a genius in the use of cavalry, who believed that by using aggressive action he could force the enemy to guard numerous points. Mosby would then attack at the weakest point, thereby ensuring numerical superiority for his troops. Although none of these units were formally referred to as Rangers, their techniques and the unique abilities they naturally possessed, combined with training and strict adherence to standards, became the groundwork of the modern-day Ranger.

WORLD WAR II

On May 26, 1942, Maj. Gen. Lucian K. Truscott, then the U.S. liaison with the British General Staff, submitted proposals to Gen. George Marshall to form an American unit along the lines of the British Commandos. The War Department agreed, and the 1st U.S. Army Ranger Battalion was formed. Truscott selected the name "Ranger" because it sounded more typically American. Maj. Gen. Russell P. Hartle, commanding all Army Forces in Northern Ireland, selected Maj. William O. Darby to lead this band of volunteers in the new battalion. On June 19, 1942, following a strenuous weeding-out program in Carrickfergus, Northern Ireland, the 1st Ranger Battalion was activated.

The training the men received—officers, noncommissioned officers, and soldiers alike—was rigorous. Of the 600 volunteers Darby brought with him, 500 survived the commando training to form the battalion. Forty-four enlisted men and five officers of this battalion participated in the Dieppe Raid with Canadian and British Commandos in 1942, becoming the first American ground soldiers to see action against the Germans in occupied Europe.

Newly promoted to lieutenant colonel, Darby inspired the Rangers to new heights. His leadership and the unit's ability were the deciding factors in their leading the North African invasion at the Port of Arzew, Algeria. The Rangers silenced two gun batteries and provided the way for the First Infantry Division to capture Oran. In Tunisia, following the invasion of North Africa, the 1st Ranger Battalion executed the first behind-the-lines raid at Sened. On March 31, 1943, they led Gen. George Patton's drive to capture the heights of El Guettar. The 12-mile night march across the rugged terrain surprised the enemy in their positions and allowed the Rangers to clear the El Guettar Pass and capture 200 prisoners in the process.

After Tunisia, the 3rd and 4th Ranger Battalions were activated and, with the 1st, spearheaded the Seventh Army landing at Gela and Licata during the Sicilian campaign that led to the capture of Messina. Performing a classic Ranger mission and wearing the colonel's eagles of his new promotion, Colonel Darby took his force, redesigned as the 6615th Ranger Force, to Anzio. This unit led the surprise night landing at the port, capturing two gun batteries, seizing the city and enlarging the beachhead before dawn, allowing the follow-on force to land uncontended.

Probably the most famous action the Rangers of the European Theater participated in was the D-Day Invasion. Under the command of Lt. Col. James E. Rudder, the 2nd Ranger Battalion assaulted the cliffs at Pointe Du Hoc, France. The daring assault of the steep cliffs allowed swift destruction of a large gun-battery positioned there. This battery provided covering fire the length of Omaha Beach and would have been devastating to the Allied forces during the assault. Then, Lt. Col. Max Schneider, commander of the 5th Ranger Battalion, landed his battalion at Omaha Beach during the June 6, 1944, invasion. It was there that the Ranger motto was first uttered. Gen. Norman D. Cota, assistant division Commander of the 29th Division, turned to Colonel Schneider and said, "Rangers, lead the way." The Rangers of

Some of the equipment used by a Ranger mortar section includes a terrain map, compass, protractor, and a Magnavox M-23 Mortar Ballistic Computer for computing and triangulating firing distances and weapon settings. Factors such as wind speed, altitude, and temperature can also be input into the computer when they might affect the accuracy of the weapon.

Rangers from the 2nd Battalion, 75th Ranger regiment, fire their Carl Gustav. When a Carl Gustav fires, its projectile is forced out the front and an equal backblast comes out the rear. These forces cancel each other out, leaving the shooter holding steady with no recoil.

The Carl Gustav is an anti-armor, shoulder-mounted weapon that fires various versions of 84 mm projectiles. Nicknamed after the person who made it, the Carl Gustav or RAWS (Ranger Anti-Armor Weapon System) provides the Rangers with the firepower they need to destroy enemy bunkers, tanks, and other fortified targets.

the European Theater were awarded the Presidential Citation, the Distinguished Unit Citation, and the Croix de Guerre for their wartime efforts.

Ranger participation extended to the Pacific Theater following the ending of hostilities in Europe. Ranger units served until the end of the war and the surrender of the Japanese on V-J Day.

The 5307th Composite Unit, Provisional, or Merrill's Marauders, was first conceived at the Quebec Conference of August 1943. Code named "Galahad," approximately 2,900 American soldiers volunteered and were formed into two combat teams consisting of two battalions each. These men, commanded by Brig. Gen. Frank D. Merrill, undertook a walk up the Ledo Road culminating in the capture of the Myitkina Airfield, the only all-weather airfield in Burma. In total, the 5307th marched more than 1,000 miles through the jungles of Burma, participated in five major and 30 minor engagements, and consistently defeated numerically superior Japanese forces. For their efforts, the unit was awarded the Presidential Unit Citation. Consolidated with the 475th Infantry on August 10, 1944, the unit was redesignated the 75th Infantry on June 21, 1954.

The Ranger tab and 2nd Ranger Battalion scroll on the left sleeve of the Ranger uniform denotes elite status within the Army. The 75th Ranger Regiment, composed of three Ranger battalions, is the premier light infantry unit of the U.S. Army. All Rangers must be airborne qualified.

Rangers are silhouetted by clouds as they stand near a smoke grenade after a combat simulation exercise. When not deployed, Rangers, like other Special Operations teams, keep up an active training schedule.

KOREA

In 1950, with the outbreak of hostilities on the Korean Peninsula, the call went out for volunteers from the Army to establish Ranger units. The implementing orders called for the formation of a headquarters unit and four companies with a target date of October 1, 1950.

These four groups arrived at Fort Benning, Georgia, on September 20, 1950. On October 9, 1950, training began with three companies of airborne-qualified men. Composing the fourth unit to begin training were former members of the 505th Airborne Infantry Regiment and the 80th Anti aircraft Artillery Battalion of the 82nd Airborne Division. Initially designated the 4th Ranger Company, they were redesignated the 2nd Ranger Infantry Company (Airborne), the only Department of the Army authorized, all-black Ranger unit in the history of the United States.

All of the volunteers were professional soldiers. Some saw service with the original Ranger Battalions, the First Special Service Force or the Office of Strategic Services during World War II. Attached as one 112-man company per 18,000-man infantry division, the Rangers fought numerous raids and ambushes, leading reconnaissance missions and spearheading assaults. Often they were used as a counterattack force to regain lost positions.

The 1st Ranger Infantry Company (Airborne) conducted a nine-mile, cross-country movement behind enemy lines to destroy an enemy complex, later identified as the Headquarters of the 12th North Korean Division. The 2nd

and 4th Ranger Companies made a combat jump at Munsan-Ni, then conducted patrols north of the 38th parallel. The 5th Ranger Company, attached to the 25th Infantry Division, held the line with Ranger sergeants commanding line infantry units. The company commander gathered up every soldier he could find during the Chinese 5th Phase Offensive to prevent the line from being breached. The 8th Ranger Infantry Company (Airborne) was attached to the 24th Infantry Division. A 33-man platoon from the 8th fought a between-the-lines battle with two Chinese reconnaissance companies. During the battle, 70 Chinese were killed and the Rangers suffered two dead and three wounded, all of whom were brought back to friendly lines.

During the Korean War, Rangers added new dimensions to tactics and concepts first devised during World War II. Rarely noted in official dispatches, the Rangers performed unique and hazardous missions for their division commanders, proudly carrying the designations and battle honors won by their predecessors in World War II.

VIETNAM

The present-day 75th Ranger Regiment is linked directly to the 13 Ranger companies of the 75th, active in Vietnam from February 1, 1969, until August 15, 1972. This time frame represents the longest sustained combat history for any American Ranger unit in more than 300 years of Ranger history. Conversion from nine infantry detachments and a company of the Indiana National Guard to Ranger Companies of the 75th Infantry began on February 1, 1969. These 13 companies conducted Ranger missions and operations for three years and seven months, every day of the 43 months while in Vietnam. Like the units and men preceding them, the current Ranger volunteers came from every branch of the Army.

Ranger companies were joined by their former adversaries, soldiers of the Vietcong and North Vietnamese Army, known as Kit Carson Scouts. These men fought alongside the Rangers and against their former units and comrades for the duration of the war. Training consisted of a combat mission for the volunteers. These volunteers were assigned to the companies but not accepted until after a series of patrols. Following the ultimate test of combat, volunteers were then allowed to wear the black beret and the red, white, and black scroll bearing the insignia of a Ranger Company.

Rangers in Vietnam were inserted into or extracted from the combat area in a variety of ways that included by foot, wheeled or tracked vehicles, air-boats, and Navy Swift Boats. The method most often used was helicopter insertions and extractions. Rangers also performed stay-behind missions, allowing a larger unit to withdraw and using the Ranger unit to occupy positions to confuse the enemy. General missions consisted of locating enemy bases and lines of communication with special, platoon-and-company-size raids. Often Ranger units were sent to conduct battle damage assessment following B-52 bombing missions.

The bulk of the Ranger volunteers were soldiers who had no opportunity to attend the Ranger School at Fort Benning. These men fought through some of the most intense patrolling actions of the Vietnam War, frequently bringing the

Rangers train to locate, attack, and secure a fortified bunker for a follow-on force. Rangers are the Army's primary force used in direct action missions—short-duration strikes to seize, destroy, capture, recover, or inflict damage on personnel or material in designated areas.

Working to secure the bunker, a Ranger demonstrates the classic squatting firing position with his M4A1 carbine. Even when using a scope, a good soldier will keep both eyes open to maintain depth perception and peripheral vision.

fight to much larger enemy forces when compromised on reconnaissance missions. Army chief of staff, Gen. Creighton Abrams, selected the 75th Rangers as the role model for the first U.S. Army Ranger units formed during peacetime.

SELECTION AND TRAINING

Though the Ranger Training School is not as famous as say, the grueling Navy SEALs BUD/S course at Coronado, the school has a staggering 65 percent dropout rate. To be a Ranger, one must be disciplined, tough, smart, in great shape, and possess superior leadership skills. A touch of fearlessness doesn't hurt either. The high dropout rate is no accident. During the 61 days of training that ranges from jungle to mountain environments, the students lose an average of 30 lbs. They are monitored by their instructors night and day, forced to overcome the rigors of mountainous and swamp operations, and are allowed to eat just once a day. By the end of training, the skinny, sunken-jawed students are often in the worst physical shape of their lives. But they also have the skill and self-confidence to be a member of the world's best light infantry strike force.

Like most of the country's other programs for Special Operations Forces, Ranger school does not admit women. But all male officers and noncommissioned officers from the United States are eligible to apply for Ranger training. Those

Waiting for a review of his team's actions after an exercise, a Ranger takes a breather alongside his weapon. Rangers are not used for operations that could be accomplished by conventional ground forces and, thus, are trained extensively to accomplish specific Special Operations missions.

A Ranger waits for instructions from a squad leader before his squad will engage a downrange target. As with all members of Special Operations Forces, each member must constantly prove and ensure he is ready for any type of mission to which he might be tasked.

RIGHT
Coming up from a trench system to provide cover for the rest of his team, a Ranger peeks up with his weapon ready. Under his watchful eyes, the rest of his team clears the trenches and bunkers of the simulated enemy.

Private First Class Jeremy Cochlin goes through an after-action review (AAR) of his squad's assault on a trench system during a live fire exercise. These reviews help teams evaluate their performance following an exercise or action to enable them to sharpen their skills even further.

Rangers receive instructions from their squad leader as they wait in a treelined area to ambush a simulated enemy force. In their role as one of the elite light infantry units in the U.S. military, Rangers are often called upon to conduct such direct action missions, which usually strike hard, but are limited in duration.

Lessons learned are not forgotten. Each time a Ranger completes an exercise, he is more ready for the next one. Training allows soldiers to make their mistakes in a safe environment, so when a real mission comes, they will be ready to perform.

Rangers advance through a trench system clearing individual lines of fire. As one soldier provides cover, others move into the next area. Here, a Ranger with an M249 SAW (Squad Automatic Weapon) covers his direction handily. A SAW in a trench can cause major problems for the enemy.

Moving down the Nisqually River, Ranger troops in Combat Rubber Raiding Crafts begin a 12-day training mission that will test their skills in many areas of operation. Rangers train in arctic, jungle, desert, and mountainous environments throughout the year.

below the rank of E-5 must get waivers from the equivalent of a lieutenant colonel (0-6 grade) in his chain of command. Before they become a member of a Ranger unit, students are expected to pass airborne school; the Ranger Training School does not require applicants to be jump qualified. Typically, about 60 percent of the school's students come from the Army, 20 percent come from other U.S. military services, and 20 percent from foreign units in allied nations. During training, rank insignia is not worn, which helps add cohesion to the group.

To get in physical shape for the harsh ten-week program, many of the students go through a one month pre-Ranger course that focuses on running and other physical training as well as basic skills such as patrolling and ambushes. While the instructors are strict—and often ornery—the students are not denied food and sleep as they are during the Ranger course.

Once the course is completed, the students start the grinding training schedule that is divided among the 4th Ranger Training Battalion at Fort Benning, Georgia; mountain training at the 5th Ranger Training Battalion at Dahlonega, Georgia; and jungle/swamp training at the 6th Ranger Training Battalion at Eglin Air Force Base, Florida. To successfully complete Ranger School, trainees must pass a total of 12 tests that range from the Army physical training test and the Ranger obstacle course, to rappelling in severe weather, an 8-mile march with a 70-pound pack, and a knot test. Students who fail to pass the tests may not sign up for Ranger school again. But those who are injured or fall ill, or who are dropped because they do not pass the classroom, exercise performance, or peer review portions of the school may try again.

The goal of Ranger school is "to produce a hardened, competent, small-unit leader who is confident he can lead his unit into combat and overcome all obstacles to accomplish his mission." The few who finish earn the right to wear the curved, yellow on black tab placed on their shoulder that says "Ranger."

During the first few days, the students process at Camp Rogers, where the Ranger Training Brigade and the 4th Ranger Training Battalion are headquartered. Next, they move on to Camp Darby, where they live in small huts in the densely wooded hills of North Carolina. A typical training day begins

Fully loaded and carrying his parachute overhead, a Ranger jumpmaster heads for the C-141. The jumpmaster is responsible for coordinating the jump operation from preparation to landing.

Second Battalion, 75th Regiment, boards an Air Force C-141 aircraft at McChord Air Force Base as they prepare for a night jump. As with all Special Operations teams, most operations will take place in darkness or in bad weather, due to the obvious concealment advantages.

with a predawn run at an eight-minute-a-mile pace at 5 A.M., and doesn't end until 2 A.M. The school places the students in a particular environment to imitate conditions of war. These "conditions" include a lack of sleep, a lack of food, extreme pressure, and of course, a grueling physical regimen.

During the Ranger Assessment Phase (RAP) at Camp Darby, each student takes the Army Physical Training Test and must perform 52 pushups in two minutes, 62 sit-ups in two minutes, a two-mile run in running shoes in less than 14:55, and six chin-ups. The trainees are expected to pass the test easily. Next, the students must complete the three-part combat water survival test, which rivals SEAL standards in terms of difficulty. First, they swim 15-meters with full gear: wearing their fatigues, boots, and web gear, including canteen and ammunition pouches, and carrying their M-16. And like SEAL trainees, the Ranger students must perform the swim without showing undue panic or fear. The student must next discard his rifle and gear while underwater, and swim to the poolside, again without revealing undue fear.

The final test is the toughest, and one that probably should not be practiced very often: Blindfolded, the trainee must walk off the end of a three meter high diving platform into a swimming pool, remove the blindfold and swim to the poolside without losing any of his equipment. If the students show the slightest hint of freaking out, the instructors might ask for a repeat performance.

With the preliminary tests finished, those who pass are assigned to companies in the 4th Ranger Training Battalion and given buddies with whom they will train and depend upon throughout the course. They are rewarded with increased physical training standards, including completing a five-mile run in 40 minutes. The students are also schooled in hand-to-hand combat, day and night land navigation techniques, and complete a series of tests known as the Ranger Stakes, which refamiliarize them with the tools of the trade.

The Ranger Stakes is made up of 11 tasks that test the trainees' ability to use light infantry and communication gear. Most of the U.S. Army soldiers are already well-familiar with the equipment, so the stakes are often routine, and a welcome respite from the demanding physical activity. The first series calls for disassembling and putting together an M-60 in a time determined by the instructor. U.S. Army soldiers must usually perform the test faster than their counterparts. The series also tests the ability to load the automatic weapon and then, to prepare a range card, which allows the weapon to be sighted. The fourth task in the stakes calls for firing an M181-A1 claymore mine. This is done by connecting the mine to a wire, and the wire to an electronic detonator. The most important part is taking cover before the mine goes off. The students then send a radio message and are tested in their abilities to encode and decode a message using the KTC 600 Operations Code. The next three tasks test the trainees' ability to maintain, correct malfunctions, and complete a functions check on the M-16, the basic weapon of the Rangers. Finally, the students must demonstrate that they can properly employ a hand grenade and maintain an M203 grenade launcher.

The trainees must pass seven of the tests. Those who fail are shown how to do the task properly, and are retested.

A Ranger squad leader guides soldiers aboard the aircraft. Their yellow parachute static lines are clearly seen here. One end of the line is attached to the ripcord on the parachute, and the other gets attached to the aircraft. When the soldier jumps, the line will unreel a short distance (allowing the free-falling soldier to safely clear the aircraft) then pull his ripcord to open the chute.

Those who fail to pass the required seven can try again in the next training class. More than nine out of ten trainees however pass the tests.

On the fourth day of training, the students get their first chance on the Darby Queen obstacle course—a 20-task course set deep in the woods. No one escapes without being covered in mud. The first task is to climb a four-meter high log fence. Next, they enter the Worm Pit, 25-meter long field crossed with barbed wire and perpetually covered in mud. The students crawl under the barbed wire on their backs—or, if the instructor so desires—they crawl through on their chests. The muddy students must then climb hand-over-hand on rafters that are, not incoincidentally, located 10 feet above another muddy pit. Slipping off is not uncommon, and those who fall are told to do it again. The final test is to climb a rope netting, grab onto a rope at the top, and slide back down. No Ranger trainee can move to the next obstacle until his buddy has also completed the task. Buddies are expected to help each other through the course.

The next morning, the students start two days of land navigation. The instructors march them to a spot outside Camp Rogers and give them a map and compass and only a few hours to arrive at the previously selected map coordinate. Getting there can mean crossing streams and climbing steep hills in adverse weather without much food or water. Each student must pass the test during the day and at night.

The Ranger Assessment Phase ends with the daunting water confidence test, which instructors claim can give a good indication of how well a trainee will perform during the rest of Ranger training—and in combat. The students are to climb 30 feet up a ladder, walk confidently across a narrow log, and then, without hesitation, drop from a rope 35 feet into Victory Pond. Finally, the soaked and shivering trainees

Still smoking from its last firing, the M224 60-mm light mortar system provides immediate indirect fire capabilities for all types of battle conditions.

climb to the top of a 60-foot tower and slide down a 200-foot rope—back into the cold water.

The next phase of Ranger training starts with a parachute jump from helicopters into a clearing. Those not airborne qualified are trucked to the site. The troops also are given classes in patrolling, leadership, and more land navigation. They learn the basics of survival, including how to catch and cook small animals, and they practice reconnaissance missions. The phase concludes with a graded four-day exercise.

During Ranger field exercises, a unit's company commander and his platoon leaders plan the mission. Because leadership abilities are a key element of Ranger training, leadership roles are rotated. Often, a student in danger of failing is given more time as leader. Depending on how he does, this courtesy can either improve his performance or speed his demise from the training school. With little food and not much sleep, the exercise is intended to gauge how the trainees react to the harshness of a war-like environment for the first time. They never know when they might be ambushed. Each day, they receive only one or two Meals Ready to Eat (MREs), which come in foil packages and contain 3,000 calories—which the students quickly burn off.

Concentration and attention to detail are stressed by instructors as factors that could save the trainee's life in combat. And during the training exercises, the lessons are pounded home. For instance, if the tired students slip up and are spotted by the enemy (usually Rangers stationed at the training battalion), they face the humiliation of being captured and placed in a makeshift prisoner of war camp. Or the students are simply "killed" when an enemy soldier registers a hit on the Military Integrated Laser Engagement System (MILES) gear that trainees wear during exercises.

By the time it is over, a large portion of the original class has quit. Many have been injured. Some decided being a Ranger was not worth the kind of intense commitment called for. Others performed poorly on evaluations and other tests. Those who make it make it this far move on to mountain school in Dahlonega, Georgia—which requires a new set of skills and the possibility of severe injury on the icy cliffs of Mt. Yonah, the highest point in Georgia.

For the first several days of mountain training, the students are allowed to build their bodies back up. They get five, sometimes six hours of sleep each day, and three meals—including two hot ones. Day and night, the training goes on. They are taught various types of knots that will secure ropes; climbing and descending techniques; and various methods of rappelling from high cliffs, including how to carry comrades along with them in case they are wounded. To pass, the students must perform three daytime rappels, including one with a full rucksack and one using only two bounces against the cliff. They must also complete a nighttime rappel while wearing their rucksacks. The field exercise is carried out much the same as it is during the other train-

A 60-mm mortar round in the hand of a Ranger. There are three basic kinds of mortar munitions: high explosive, smoke, and illumination.

A Ranger is suited up in static line parachute gear for a night jump. Rangers often use night jumps as a means of insertion into areas not accessible by other methods.

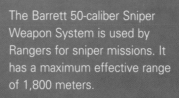
The Barrett 50-caliber Sniper Weapon System is used by Rangers for sniper missions. It has a maximum effective range of 1,800 meters.

The M4A1 carbine, which has a collapsible stock, is ideal for trench and mountain warfare situations, and has thus become a standard in the Special Operations community.

The M249 SAW (Squad Automatic Weapon) , a superb light machine gun for immediate suppression use.

Ranger gun crews are issued the 9 mm Berretta M9 pistol as a standard sidearm for their secondary weapon to use in personal defense.

For their next firing sequence, members of a Ranger mortar team acting as the Fire Direction Center (FDC) work to obtain proper range, distance, and firing computations for the gunners. These strikes will provide accurate fire support for Rangers downrange.

ing phases. It usually begins with an airborne jump, although this time, the landing targets are smaller and include trees. While the students continue their long training runs and steady diet of flutter kicks and push-ups, most of the dropouts in the mountain phase succumb to injury, not failure to complete the required tasks. Few escape without at least minor sprains and dislocations. After it is over, another 10 percent of the original group has been left behind.

The survivors board a bus to Eglin Air Force Base for jungle training in the mosquito-infested swamps of the Florida panhandle. The mood on the bus is often celebratory. The trainees know that the toughest part is behind them. But the instructors know that some of the toughest training also lies ahead. Jungle training starts with a class on avoiding snakes and other harmful reptiles and what to do if bitten. And then, for nine days they live in the swamps, often with wet clothes and the smell of the jungle permeating their bodies. Again, food and sleep become limited. They also learn the classic Ranger tactic called movement-to-contact, which is perhaps best described as an infantry-meets-guerrilla-warfare tactic, in which students learn how to move through enemy territory, make contact, and then disengage again. The students also learn how to properly cross streams and are taught small boat operations in the swamps. Finally, the field training exercises put everything together in a neat package. In the dark of night, the students load their Zodiacs and set off for Santa Rosa Island, located in the Gulf of Mexico. After they reach shore, they fight a simulated battle, and if they perform well, they eventually capture the island.

As difficult as Ranger School is, it should be no surprise that over the years, many deaths have occurred during training. Students have been killed during parachute and climbing accidents, while others have drowned while crossing fast-flowing mountain streams and tidal swamps. There is also the danger of weather extremes, including the frequent lightning strikes over the Florida panhandle. The dangers were underscored in February 1995 when four Ranger students died and four others were hospitalized after spending hours in cold, chest-high swamp water at Eglin Air Force Base. The Army said the men had been in the field for six days at the time of their deaths and were in the process of building a bridge in the hardwood swamps when they succumbed to hypothermia.

Those who successfully complete each of the phases and graduate the morning after jungle training ends, are survivors. Literally. And for those who still have a yearning for the trials and tribulations of Ranger training, the Army also offers a five-week long-range surveillance unit leaders course for NCOs and officers. The course, also offered by the 4th Ranger Training Battalion, trains Rangers in long-range surveillance, including countertracking and stalking. The highlight, if it can be called that, is for the Rangers to use a map to find a hidden cache of food—or get nothing to eat.

A Ranger heads down an embankment of the Nisqually River.

Waiting to hear the review of their actions from their commanding officer, Rangers stand in silence on a training range. Reviews such as these will enable these Rangers to more accurately gauge their performance as individuals and as a team.

ORGANIZATION

As is true with most of the nation's other Special Operations units, the 75th Ranger Regiment's 2,000 soldiers are members of the Joint Special Operations Command. Along with the Army's Green Berets, Delta, and other units, they are part of the U.S. Army Special Operations Command.

The 75th consists of three battalions: the 1st at Hunter Army Air Field, Georgia; the 2nd at Fort Lewis, Washington; and the 3rd at Fort Benning. The regimental headquarters are at Fort Benning, headed by a colonel. Ranger battalions have 580 soldiers divided among three combat companies, a battalion headquarters, and a headquarters company that includes a fire support team and medical and communications sections. Each company has three rifle platoons with 152 Rangers each and a weapons platoon that has about 22 men. The rifle platoons are divided into three squads and a machine gun squad. Squad leaders are at least staff sergeants. All team, squad, and platoon leaders learn basic first aid and how to administer intravenous injections to prevent shock. Each squad also has a medic—who also carries a rifle.

The Ranger mission is multifaceted. As the world's best light infantry unit force, they can operate on any terrain in any climate. They are capable of light infantry tasks as well as Special Operations missions. They can deploy by launching an airborne strike, by helicopter, or boat. Each Ranger battalion rotates on a monthly basis as the Ranger Ready Force, meaning it will be ready to deploy anywhere in the world within 18 hours. At least once a year, each battalion holds a surprise readiness exercise in which they prepare for a mission, including loading onto C-130s and preparing for a jump. The men often do not know whether the exercise is real or simply training.

Rangers are constantly ready to operate in any environment. They train in jungle, mountain, and desert environments at least

A Ranger squad, armed and ready, waits on an embankment for the command to move out. Two squads are to travel in Combat Rubber Raiding Crafts to an objective three miles downstream. River operations are just one of the multitude of environments the Rangers train in to enable them to be deployed by the National Command Authority to any area in the world.

Maintaining a high degree of readiness, Rangers train with a number of live-fire exercises like this one. As one officer put it, "Playing with blanks is one thing, but live ammunition instills respect for instructions and solidifies a soldier's resolve to complete the mission correctly and effectively."

once each year and in simulated urban locales once every six months. At least two of every three years, they also train in the extreme cold and on amphibious operations. And when they are not practicing for missions, Ranger units engage in the most intense physical training regimen in the Army: five days a week, 48 weeks a year, all at the Ranger pace of eight minutes per mile.

EQUIPMENT

With few exceptions, the weapons used by Rangers are the same as most Army infantry units. The M-16, fitted with an M203 40-mm grenade launcher, is the basic weapon, and the M60 is the standard machine gun. Ranger units are also equipped with 60-mm mortars and 84-mm Ranger Antitank Weapons Systems (RAWS).

One problem that continues to nag Ranger units is the necessity for them to tote heavy loads on missions because they are often not sure when they will be resupplied. It is not unusual for members of this "light" infantry force to tote more than 100 pounds of gear. The heavy loads, which include everything from extra ammunition to three days' supply of food and water, can be particularly hazardous during airborne drops—a method of insertion Rangers employ quite frequently.

The problem of heavy loads is not new. According to *Rangers at War*, by Shelby L. Stanton, during the Vietnam War, the following is only a sampling of the gear lugged around by a six-member Ranger team: Two PRC-25 radios, spare radio batteries, one Starlight scope, one M79 grenade launcher, one XM21 rifle with sniper scope, one M60 machine gun, one pair of binoculars, four M79 light antitank weapons, 1,500 rounds of M60 ammunition, 300 M-14 rounds, and more than a dozen flares and grenades. Additionally, each member carried an M-16 and ammunition, eight quarts of water, six grenades, two claymore mines, and other gear.

In addition to basic equipment, today's Rangers also have the most modern tools, including infrared aiming devices and night vision equipment. The AN/PVS-4 night vision individual weapons sight can mount on M-16s, M60s, M79 grenade launchers, and other weapons, or it can be hand-held. This high-tech gadget's range is up to 600 meters

Beginning the initial assault upon a fortified bunker, a Ranger lays suppressive fire upon a suspected enemy position as other troops flanking him advance downrange toward the intended target.

A Ranger reviews the various elements of his parachute rig before strapping it on and making last-minute adjustments for a night training jump. Every detail is important when working with a parachute.

in moonlight and 300 meters in starlight. Many Rangers also sport night vision goggles. The AN/PVS-5 night vision goggles are lightweight and battery powered and include a built-in infrared source. Their range is 150 meters in moonlight and 50 meters in starlight. The latest model is the AN/PVS-7b, which allow Rangers to see clearer images in lower light levels.

One of the Rangers' most important training tools is MILES gear, short for Military Integrated Laser Engagement System. MILES equipment, which runs on batteries, is used with M-16s and M60s. One part of MILES fits over the barrel of the weapon with a blank adapter, and the other part—a sensor—is worn by the Ranger. When the weapon fires the blank, the laser is activated and if the aim is true, the sensor on the "enemy" makes a high-pitched beeping sound and he is considered killed or wounded.

Finally, there is the Ranger Handbook, a pocket-sized pamphlet filled with everything a Ranger needs to know, from various combat tactics to survival tips in extreme weather to the use of explosives. Most Rangers are issued the booklet during training school, and keep it handy as a way to brush up on their techniques.

A Ranger waits with his automatic weapon as the squad decides the next course of action to take. They are trying to locate a predetermined ambush point during an exercise.

A Forward Observer (FO) relays his position and distance to the target to a nearby mortars team. Once the mortars triangulate the target's position, shells will rain on it with deadly accuracy.

MISSIONS

Abrams' vision laid the groundwork for the present-day Ranger Regiment. "The Ranger Battalion is to be an elite, light and the most proficient infantry battalion in the world," Abrams said, "A battalion that can do things with its hands and weapons better than anyone. The battalion will contain no hoodlums or brigands; and if the battalion were formed from such persons, it would be disbanded. Wherever the battalion goes, it will be apparent that it is the best."

Because of Abrams' desire, the 1st Battalion (Ranger), 75th Infantry was officially activated at Fort Stewart, Georgia. The 2nd Battalion soon followed, being stationed at Fort Lewis, Washington, on October 1, 1974. This farsightedness proved to be fortunate. In October 1983, the Ranger battalions were deployed to protect the lives of American citizens living and studying on the island of Grenada. Under the code name Urgent Fury, the 1st and 2nd Battalions conducted a parachute assault to seize the airfield at Point Salines. They further conducted air assault operations to eliminate any pockets of resistance remaining, following the safe extraction of all students at the True Blue Medical Campus. This action was instrumental in the formation of the 75th Ranger Regiment and the 3rd Battalion, 75th Ranger Regiment, both headquartered at Fort Benning, Georgia. The 1st and 2nd

Battalions were redesignated, joining the largest force of Rangers, more than 2,000, since World War II.

The regiment received its colors October 3, 1984. A scant five years later, Rangers again were thrust in the forefront of American intervention. During Operation Just Cause, the entire Regiment participated in restoring democracy to Panama. Rangers spearheaded the action by conducting two, parachute assaults to secure airfields for follow-on forces. The 1st Battalion, reinforced by C Company, 3rd Battalion and a regimental combat and control team, parachuted onto Omar Torrijos International Airport and Tocumen Military Airfield. Their mission was to secure the airfield for the arrival of the 82nd Airborne Division and neutralize the threat presented by the Panamanian Defense Forces, 2nd Rifle Company. The 2nd and 3rd Battalions, with an RCCT, conducted a parachute assault onto the airfield at Rio Hato to neutralize the PDF 6th and 7th Rifle Companies. An additional task was seizing Gen. Manuel Noriega's beach house. Both operations were successful, allowing the Ranger Regiment to capture 1,014 prisoners of war and more than 18,000 weapons of various types. Forty-two Rangers were wounded, and five Rangers died.

In 1991, Rangers again answered the nation's call, deploying a company from 2nd Battalion, 75th Ranger

A Ranger waits for orders over the radio as a result of a sudden change of battle objectives. Rangers thrive on the ability to adapt to changing combat conditions.

The definitive black beret of the U.S. Army Rangers and Ranger tab and 75th Ranger Regiment scroll. Since their beginning, Rangers have made a habit of leading the way—from blowing rail links behind enemy lines during the Civil War to scaling 100-foot cliffs while under fire during the D-Day landings in Normandy. More recently, the United States has called on them to perform a dizzying variety of tasks, including long-range reconnaissance missions, taking down enemy airports, and even stalking foreign leaders.

Rangers discuss a strategy for an ambush as they quietly wait behind a treeline for a simulated enemy patrol to cross. Like any elite light infantry force, ambushing patrols is a task for which Rangers are well suited. Other light infantry missions include securing airfields, short-duration reconnaissance, and destroying communications and command and control facilities.

A commanding officer gives instructions to a Ranger subordinate to pass on to his squad as they provide security for a hilltop command post.

Regiment to Saudi Arabia in support of Operation Desert Storm. Their subsequent missions upheld the proud Ranger traditions of the past and led to the overall success of the operation to secure Kuwait against the forces of Saddam Hussein.

Much has been written about Task Force Ranger and the decisions made by the National Command Authority and the leaders on the ground. The men of the 3rd Battalion, 75th

Ranger Regiment were deployed to Mogadishu, Somalia, to render aid to the people of that region. Their actions were executed under the most austere and challenging circumstances, and they lived up to the traditions of the Rangers, past and present, supporting the United Nations operations from August 22, 1993, to October 25, 1993. Specialist John H. Stebbins, one of the 30 Rangers wounded in Somalia said, "Every Ranger wants to be over there. It's not that we have a

RANGER CREED

Recognizing that I volunteered as a Ranger, fully knowing the hazards of my chosen profession, I will always endeavor to uphold the prestige, honor, and high esprit de corps of the Rangers.

Acknowledging the fact that a Ranger is a more elite soldier who arrives at the cutting edge of battle by land, sea, or air, I accept the fact that as a Ranger my country expects me to move further, faster, and fight harder than any other soldier.

Never shall I fail my comrades. I will always keep myself mentally alert, physically strong, and morally straight; and I will shoulder more than my share of the task whatever it may be. One hundred percent and then some.

Gallantly will I show the world that I am a specially selected and well-trained soldier. My courtesy to superior officers, neatness of dress, and care of equipment shall set the example for others to follow.

Energetically will I meet the enemies of my country. I shall defeat them on the field of battle for I am better trained and will fight with all my might. Surrender is not a Ranger word. I will never leave a fallen comrade to fall into the hands of the enemy and under no circumstances will I ever embarrass my country.

Readily will I display the intestinal fortitude to fight on to the Ranger objective and complete the mission, though I be the lone survivor. **Rangers, Lead The Way!**

blood-lust or anything, it's just that we want to be there watching out for our buddies."

The firefight at Mogadishu accounted for the six Silver Stars, 30 Bronze Stars, 39 Bronze Stars with 'V,' or Valor, devices, and 30 Purple Hearts awarded to the Rangers of Task Force Ranger. The most important, though, in the eyes of all Rangers is the Valorous Unit Award presented them by Gen. Hugh Shelton for their service in Somalia. General Shelton, commander of the U.S. Special Operations Command, located at MacDill Air Force Base, Florida, spoke of the sacrifices made during the battle in Mogadishu. He described the intense firefight, the battle to relieve the members of Task Force Ranger, and finally of the Rangers who made the supreme sacrifice. The whole event, and the entire story of the Ranger, is summed up with the last stanza of the Ranger Creed, and that, in itself, speaks the story of the 75th Ranger Regiment.

"Readily will I display the intestinal fortitude required to fight on to the Ranger objective and complete the mission, though I be the lone survivor. Rangers, Lead The Way!"

TOP RIGHT
In advance of the arrival of a Ranger squad, a Ranger collects the oars on a CRRC to prepare it for an advance on an objective. Once the squad arrives, they will quickly board it and head downstream.

A Ranger squad walks along the banks of the Nisqually River moving toward their objective. Noted for their ability to navigate their way out of any environment, Rangers have been called the best light infantry force in the world.

A night vision lens shows U.S. Army Rangers fast roping from a Blackhawk helicopter on the outskirts of Mogadishu, Somalia, during combat operations in Operation Restore Hope. *U.S. Army*

CHAPTER THREE THE ARMY SPECIAL FORCES

Today's Special Forces soldiers, world-renowned for their tactical and diplomatic skills, are the ultimate Renaissance soldiers. Trained in a variety of military skills, they also build hospitals and schools, aid famine and hurricane victims, and operate on wounded personnel with the same skill as an advanced medical school student. Identified by a distinctive green beret, it has earned Special Forces the common title, the Green Berets.

The term "Special Forces" was first used during World War II and referred to the British National Operations organization. Later it became Special Forces Headquarters when the British army's Special Operations Executive and the U.S. Office of Strategic Services joined forces. Army's Special Forces evolved through a spirited heritage spanning three centuries and threading itself through numerous organizations.

This heritage is evident in its insignia. A gold and teal arrowhead-shaped Special Forces patch represents the craft and stealth of Native Americans, America's first warriors. An upturned dagger is superimposed on the arrowhead and represents the unconventional warfare missions of Special Forces. The three lightning bolts crossing the dagger represent blinding speed and strength, and the three methods of infiltration—land, sea, and air. The gold represents constancy and inspiration, and the background of teal blue stands for Special Forces' encompassing all branch assignments.

Army Special Forces snipers—dressed in ghillie suits to blend in with their surrounding environment—take aim on targets 800–1,000 meters away. Sniper training through the U.S. Army John F. Kennedy Special Warfare School and Center at Fort Bragg is one of only two sniper programs within the Department of Defense that produces Category I snipers. The other is the Marine Corps Scout Sniper Instructor Course at Quantico, Virginia. Both courses qualify graduates as highly trained snipers capable of instructing their peers.

A view of the well-known Army Special Forces green beret and Special Forces and Airborne tabs and insignia worn on dress uniforms. The writing on the flash of the beret bears their Latin motto *De Oppresson Liber*, which means "To Free the Oppressed." The Army's Special Forces, known popularly as the Green Berets, are America's main weapon for waging unconventional warfare in an age where conventional conflicts have become increasingly rare.

Prominent to the distinctive black and silver crest worn by Special Forces soldiers is their motto: *de Oppresso Liber*, a Latin phrase that means *To Free the Oppressed*. The two crossed arrows symbolize the role of the Special Forces in unconventional warfare and reflect the qualities of the Special Forces soldier—straight and true. An upturned knife represents the one issued to members of the First Special Service Force.

HISTORY

Special Forces' heritage starts with Rogers' Rangers from the French and Indian War in Colonial America. They used the tactics of Native Americans, often fighting in small numbers where

1st Lt. James R. Rondeau (C Co., 2nd Battn, 19th SFG-A), uses a computer during a test of his skills in an Arabic language class at Fort Bragg, North Carolina. Unlike other Special Operations teams, members of the Army's Special Forces are required to be fluent in a second language. Fluency in the national language of a foreign country can be a great asset to a team operating there.

During Special Operations Target Interdiction, soldiers training to be Category I snipers take aim on targets 400 meters away. Sniper training is six weeks in length and is broken down into seven subject areas. Besides advanced rifle and sniper marksmanship, the course stresses the ballistic characteristics and the effect that the environment has on the path and terminal impact of the bullet.

regular army units would not go. The tradition continued in the Revolutionary War with Francis Marion, the South Carolina "Swamp Fox." His tactics of harassment hampered the British army's exploits in the south. During the Civil War, John Mosby's band of Confederate raiders cut union lines of supplies and communications. After the Civil War the official formation of the U.S. Scouts carried on the heritage as its members, Native American Indians, assisted in the settlement of the American West. Their courage and perseverance earned them 16 Medals of Honor.

It was World War II that brought today's Special Forces units into a lasting reality. Special Forces soldiers trace their lineage directly to the First Special Service Force, "The Devil's Brigade," a joint Canadian-American unit that fought in Italy and France, and the 5307th Composite Unit (Provisional), or "Merrill's Marauders," who fought the Japanese for control of Southeast Asia. Special Forces' heritage also includes the Ranger Battalions that fought in the European Theater in such actions as found in North Africa.

Perhaps no other World War II unit though was more responsible for today's Special Forces than the Office of

Strategic Services, the OSS. Formed in 1941 as the Coordinator of Intelligence under Col. William Donovan (Wild Bill), a WW I Medal of Honor recipient, the unit became the OSS in 1942. One of the primary missions of the OSS was the Jedburgh Mission. It consisted of dropping three-man teams into France, Belgium, and Holland, where they linked up with partisan movements, trained them, and conducted guerrilla operations against the Germans in preparation for the D-Day invasion.

The OSS also deployed Detachment 101 to assist Gen. Joseph Stillwell's forces in Burma. It gathered intelligence, conducted special reconnaissance missions, trained guerrilla forces, and conducted direct action missions against the Japanese, which resulted in more than 10,000 Japanese dead with a loss of 206 of its own. In the occupied Philippine Islands, Captain Volckmann and Lieutenant Colonel Fertig were organizing the remains of the Filipino Army, and natives, into guerrilla forces and intelligence networks. After World War II, then Colonels Volckmann, Fertig and Aaron Bank, a former OSS operative, were instrumental in ensuring that guerrilla

An Arabic language instructor works with two Special Forces team members as they go through their classroom portion of an Arabic language class at Fort Bragg, North Carolina. Languages taught to soldiers are specific to their global area of operation. These soldiers will be attached to the 5th Special Forces Group (Airborne), which serves the Middle East region.

Called the Vertical Wind Tunnel, this building at Fort Bragg, North Carolina, simulates a free-fall environment for year-round military paratrooper training. Upward winds produced in the tunnel simulate a free-fall rate of up to 200 feet per second. This controlled environment allows instructors, as seen here in black jump suits, to monitor a student's technique and make hands-on adjustments during their "flight."

warfare was a major component of unconventional operations leading to the formation of today's Special Forces.

During the Korean conflict, the 8086th Army Unit was formed. It controlled all partisan operations within the Korean peninsula, including direct action missions; establishment of escape and evasion routes; establishment of stay-behind bases; and, sabotage and intelligence gathering missions. During this time, Bank went to Fort Bragg, North Carolina, to form a 2,300-man unit that would become the first Special Forces unit. On June 19, 1952, the 10th Special Forces Group was activated, with Bank as its commander. The group later split. One-half remained as the 10th and deployed to West Germany, where it became responsible for special operations in the Europe. The other half became the 77th Special Forces Group and remained at Fort Bragg.

The French withdrawal from Southeast Asia and the growing influence of communist forces there helped bring about the introduction of Special Forces soldiers to that part of the world. Operational detachments from the 77th were eventually sent to Thailand, Taiwan, and then to Vietnam in 1956. In 1957, these detachments became the 1st Special Forces Group, which was responsible for the Far Eastern theater of operations.

In the early 1960s, Special Forces grew at a rate unthinkable by its founders. By 1963, with President John F. Kennedy's interest and belief in their capabilities, the 77th had become the 7th Special Forces Group. The 5th, 8th, 6th, and 3rd Groups were also activated. At this time, two National Guard units, the 19th and 20th Special Forces Groups, were activated.

The 5th Special Forces Group became the primary group responsible for actions in Vietnam. Besides direct action and strategic reconnaissance missions, Special Forces soldiers were responsible for training more than 60,000 tribesmen in modern warfare techniques. They also conducted operations designed to "win the hearts and minds" of the Vietnamese

population. Special Forces soldiers built schools, hospitals, and government buildings. They provided medical care to civilians, assisted in dredging canals and other civil-military assistance missions. Special Forces soldiers also created and taught the Military Assistance Command, Vietnam, Recondo School that was responsible for training both U.S. and South Vietnamese soldiers in long-range reconnaissance missions.

War-fighting military operations were the primary missions of Special Forces soldiers. During their 14-year involvement in Vietnam, Special Forces soldiers earned 17 Medals of Honor. In fact, the first MOH awarded for heroism in Vietnam was earned by a Special Forces captain, Roger H.C. Donlon, in 1964. Donlon led the successful defense of Nam Dong against a Viet Cong attack while sustaining a mortar wound to his stomach.

Perhaps though, Special Forces' single most daring action in Vietnam was the raid on the Son Tay prisoner of war camps outside Hanoi. After months of planning and training, the rescue attempt was made on November 18, 1970. The raiders, all hand-picked and led by Col. Arthur "Bull" Simons, infiltrated into North Vietnam from Thailand by helicopters while Navy jets conducted diversionary raids. Upon arriving at the camp, and eliminating the guard forces there, the American raiders learned that the POWs had recently been moved. Twenty-seven minutes after arriving, all of the raiders left. In the United States, the planning and execution of the raid became very controversial, while in North Vietnam, the raid is credited with improving the life of American POWs. The Son Tay mission remains a classical model for the planning and execution of raids and continues to be taught by the United States and other countries when planning special operation raids.

In March 1971, 5th Special Forces Group returned to Fort Bragg and the SF mission in Vietnam came to a halt. The 1st, 3rd, 6th, and 8th Groups were deactivated and the missions of Special Forces changed to reflect a new Army emphasis on conventional war-fighting methods. In order to keep Special Forces alive, its leaders took the lessons learned in Vietnam in nation building and helped to build roads and medical clinics in the United States, and staffed free medical clinics.

SELECTION AND TRAINING

Special Forces training emphasizes team work as well as individual ingenuity; requires mental alertness and physical grit, and commitment. The training lasts for more than a year, and includes learning one of the four Special Forces' military occupational specialties and foreign language training. Applicants to the Special Forces must be male Army soldiers who are airborne qualified by the time they enter the Special Forces Qualification Course.

The toughest part physically, is the first phase of training, the Special Forces Assessment and Selection program. This

An Army Special Forces SERE (Survival, Escape, Resistance, and Evasion) instructor demonstrates hand-to-hand combat techniques with a SERE course student. This survival course is one of many specialized courses within the U.S. Army John F. Kennedy Special Warfare Center and School.

program allows assessors to evaluate each soldier's physical performance, creativity, motivation, ability to handle stress, and ability to work individually or as a team member. The 21-day course is divided into three phases. Phase one is designed to evaluate a soldier's emotional and psychological makeup, which is done through a battery of written and practical tests. Phase two tests the soldier's endurance and physical strength. The soldier is required to complete a range of physical tests that include an obstacle course, long rucksack marches, timed runs, swimming while in uniform and boots, day and night land navigation, and more psychological tests. To further test their abilities to work in a high-stress environment, candidates are subjected to sleep deprivation as part of their evaluation. Phase three is designed to assess the soldier's leadership abilities, and determine how well he performs as part of a team. As the team leader, a soldier will be assessed on his military skills and on his ability to motivate his team to accomplish a given task.

A board of impartial and senior officers and NCOs reviews the soldier's overall performance during the course. They also make the final determination as to whether the soldier is suitable for Special Forces training and identify the

specific Special Forces military occupational specialty for which he will be trained. The 50 percent who either quit or are rejected are sent back to their regular units. Many of them often return and try out for Special Forces again.

After successfully completing the SFAS, the soldier is then recommended for the Special Forces Qualification Course. The Special Forces Qualification Course, or "Q Course," is divided into three phases. Phase I, is common skills training such as land navigation, patrolling, and leadership.

Phase II is training in the soldier's military occupational specialty and is based on his background, aptitude, and desires. Enlisted soldiers may select from four Special Forces military occupational skills. All courses are taught at Fort Bragg and last from 13 to 45 weeks. These include Special Forces Weapons Sergeant's course; Special Forces Engineer Sergeant's course; Special Forces Medical Sergeant's course; and, Special Forces Communications Sergeant's course. Officers, including Warrant officers, attend a separate series of classes.

Special Forces Weapons sergeant training emphasizes light and heavy infantry weapons, antiarmor weapons, and operations training related to the weapons sergeant's duties

With his name written in both English and Arabic on a sign hanging from his desk, a Special Forces team member attends the classroom portion of an Arabic language class at Fort Bragg, North Carolina. Many are fluent in more than just the two languages required.

on a Special Forces Operational Detachment, more commonly called an A-team. Students learn to recognize and use a wide variety of foreign-made weapons from both allied and hostile nations, as well as U.S.–made weapons. Training with U.S. weapons includes obsolete items prevalent among Third World nations that have received military assistance from the United States. Their tactical training also includes small-unit tactics of both the U.S. and foreign armies.

Engineer sergeant students receive instruction in a wide variety of explosives—U.S. military and civilian, foreign-made, and "homemade." The engineer student also learns engineer rigging and construction techniques, which enable an A-Team to assist indigenous populations: to build housing, schools, and hospitals; install practical and safe sanitation; install potable water and electrical systems; grade roads and build bridges. Students learn to use various construction materials and tools.

The Special Forces medical sergeant course is the longest of the Special Forces MOS qualification courses. It enables the Special Forces medic to provide medical and veterinary care in operational situations where usual health care professionals, military or civilian, are not available. Students are trained in advanced life-saving skills, surgical and advanced trauma, anatomy, physiology, pharmacology, dental science, basic emergency medical skills, and veterinary medicine. Medical sergeant students use the latest educational technology, including long-distance learning through the Internet. Before graduation, students get hands-on training with emergency trauma units in New York City.

A Special Forces communications sergeant student, in conjunction with his MOS training, learns to operate and maintain several types of radios using a wide variety of antennas and other systems. He learns techniques needed to transmit messages over long distances and avoid signal detection by the enemy. Students are required to gain a proficiency in the use of International Morse Code and in voice and radio transmission procedures. Students develop their skills not only in the classroom, but in rugged terrain, using "real-world" atmospheric conditions and distances.

Special Forces noncommissioned officers volunteer for warrant officer training. As warrant officer students, they receive classes that capitalize on their previous Special Forces experience. After their graduation from the Warrant Officer Candidate School, the newly appointed Warrant Officers attend the 18-week-long Special Forces Warrant Officer Basic Course. Classes cover such subjects as leadership, management, advanced Special Operations techniques, and managing training and operations. The training goal is to make the students' "subject matter experts" in tactical and technical special operations.

The Special Forces Detachment Officer Course qualifies officers to serve as Special Forces detachment commanders. In addi-

Using the method of "learning by association," common items are laid out in an Arabic language class. The 14 language classes taught range from 18 to 25 weeks in duration. The Arabic class is one of the longest, at 24 weeks and 2 days.

tion to learning planning and leadership techniques necessary to direct and employ special operations experts on their teams, students learn principles, strategies, and tactics of unconventional warfare, foreign internal defense, strike operations, and strategic reconnaissance, which are the missions of Special Forces. Students also learn other Special Operations activities, such as

An Army Special Forces soldier assists an Argentinean soldier with the operation of radios and other electronic equipment at an Argentinean command post in Panama. In their roles as teachers, Special Forces soldiers will teach their skills to the forces of friendly countries. The Argentineans' goal is to learn how to better defend and protect their country by utilizing training resources provided by the United States.

RIGHT
With an Argentinean soldier following close behind, an Army Special Forces A-Team soldier walks a treeline. The soldier packs an M4A1 carbine in the jungles of Panama.

Darting up quickly to cross the road, a Special Forces A-Team soldier teaches the finer points of the maneuver to Argentinean troops. The soldiers are participating in the Cabanas '97 exercise, which brings armies from four Central American countries together to learn from the elite American soldiers.

LEFT
Watching from the cover of the jungle, a Special Forces A-Team soldier waits for an opportune moment to cross a road.

Squinting up into the driving rain, a group of Special Forces SERE school students watch a demonstration being given by an instructor. Other Special Operations Forces members will often go through the SERE school at Fort Bragg, too.

psychological operations and civil affairs. They undergo the same rigorous physical training and stress situations as the enlisted students and become thoroughly familiar with NCO skills.

In addition to MOS specific training, the Q-course includes land navigation, small unit tactics, air operations, mission planning, and for officers, survival, evasion, resistance, and escape skills. Because a Special Forces soldier must be able to assist his team members, cross-training is conducted in the qualification courses.

Phase III training begins with air operations and mission planning and execution. Students from all the MOS courses come together to form A-teams. Here they are tested on

their knowledge, their ability to work in realistic conditions, and how well they work with others of different backgrounds in order to accomplish their mission. The soldiers are deployed to the Uwharrie National Forest in central North Carolina for a three-week, unconventional warfare exercise called "Robin Sage. "There, as a member of an A-team, soldiers are evaluated on their specialties, common skills, and teamwork. Robin Sage is carefully monitored by veteran Special Forces members, who assess the performance of the candidates.

Robin Sage is made as realistic as possible, with local civilians playing the role of contacts. The scenario has an

Moving through the jungles of Panama, a Special Forces soldier plans tactics for a patrol with a member of the Argentinean army. During this exercise, they are defending a higher ground command post and landing zone from other soldiers from Bolivia and Paraguay participating in the exercise.

Standing in a heavy rain, SERE school students watch an instructor rappel from a concrete wall before the students will attempt to try it themselves. The weather has to be pretty severe to cancel this school for the day.

One armed with a spotting scope and the other with the weapon, Army Special Forces snipers dressed in ghillie suits look downrange toward their target. These highly trained marksmen will often have to wait long periods of time for their target to come into their sights, and in a majority of cases, they only get one shot.

opposing force, a guerrilla force, and a civilian auxiliary. As occurs in real-world missions, the students carry everything they need: weapons, radios, rations, extra boots and clothes, and other field items. An average rucksack may weigh up to 100 pounds.

After successfully completing all three phases of the Special Forces Qualification Course, soldiers are awarded the Special Forces tab and their first Green Beret. They are then assigned to a Special Forces group. Before going to their designated group, students attend foreign language training, which is also conducted at Fort Bragg. The language each candidate learns depends upon the Special Forces group to which he is assigned. Language training courses may be as long as six months. After completion of the language training, new Special Forces soldiers report to assigned groups, but this does not mean that their training is complete. In fact, it may just be starting. Training continues throughout their careers. Depending on unit requirements, Special Forces soldiers train in one of the advanced skills, such as military free-fall, combat diver, special operations target interdiction, survival, evasion, resistance and escape, and water infiltration.

ORGANIZATION

U.S. Army Special Forces Command, headquartered at Fort Bragg and commanded by a two-star general, exercises command and control of five active-duty Special Forces groups,

and also exercises training oversight over two National Guard groups. Its mission is to train, validate and prepare Special Forces units to deploy and execute operational requirements for the war-fighting commanders-in-chief. Special Forces Command is subordinate to the U.S. Army Special Operations Command (USASOC). A three-star general commands USASOC, which is headquartered at Fort Bragg. USASOC oversees the Special Forces, Rangers, Special Operations aviation, Civil Affairs and Psychological Operations, Special Operations Support units, and the U.S. Army John F. Kennedy Special Warfare Center and School.

Each Special Forces Group is regionally oriented to support one of the war-fighting commanders-in-chief. Special Forces soldiers routinely deploy in support of U.S. European Command, U.S. Atlantic Command, U.S. Pacific Command, U.S. Southern Command, and the U.S. Central Command. The five Special Forces groups and their areas of responsibility are as follows: the 1st Special Forces Group based at

During the Robin Sage field training exercise, a sort of 14-day final exam for Army Special Forces students, an SF captain breaks out a set of bagpipes and begins playing them at a remote command post just before breakfast. This and other oddities are intended to throw the students mindset and concentration off and is also a security violation that students are expected to confront.

A SERE instructor demonstrates a type of shelter that can be built above ground and between trees in swamp areas or streambeds where it is too wet for a ground-based shelter.

TOP LEFT
A Special Forces SERE (Survival, Evasion, Resistance, and Escape) school instructor demonstrates to students one of the many types of small animal traps that can be made from common items when needed for survival. Soldiers are also taught what kinds of plants are safe to eat, basic first aid, how to build shelters, and other combat survival techniques.

A sign at the entrance to the SERE course at Fort Bragg, North Carolina, warns of its restricted nature.

Fort Lewis, Washington, and Okinawa, Japan—the Pacific and Eastern Asia; the 3rd Special Forces Group based at Fort Bragg—the Caribbean and Western Africa; the 5th Special Forces Group based at Fort Campbell, Kentucky—Southwest Asia and Northeastern Africa; the 7th Special Forces Group also based at Fort Bragg, and Fort Davis, Panama—Central and South America; the 10th Special Forces Group based at Fort Carson, Colorado, and Stuttgart, Germany—Europe and Western Asia.

Each Special Forces group has three battalions, a headquarters company, and a support company. Each of the three battalions has three companies and a headquarters company. In a Special Forces company, there are six A-teams. One of the six A-teams is trained in combat diving and one is trained in military free-fall parachuting. Both are methods of infiltration.

The A-team is the fundamental building block for all Special Forces groups. A captain leads the 12-man team. Second in command is a warrant officer. Two noncommissioned officers, and eight soldiers trained in each of the five Special Forces functional areas—weapons, engineer, medical, communications, and operations and intelligence—compose the remainder of the team.

Army Special Forces soldiers in training to be Category I snipers take aim on targets downrange as they train on base at Fort Bragg in North Carolina. Sniper training through the base's John F. Kennedy Special Warfare School and Center teaches these soldiers the fine art of marksmanship and the incredible concentration, technique, and ballistic knowledge that must accompany each shot.

A Special Forces soldier writes down his score that was radioed back to him from the target area. Accurate shots recorded from a range of distances become the basis for a passing grade during the sniper course training.

All team members are Special Forces and airborne qualified, and cross-trained in different skills, as well as being multilingual.

Capabilities of the highly versatile A-team include planning and conducting SF operations separately or as part of a larger force; infiltrating and exfiltrating an area undetected by air, land, or sea; and conducting operations in remote areas. At times, the A-team must wosrk in hostile environments for extended periods of time with a minimum of supervision and support. Its members organize, equip, train, and advise indigenous forces on small unit tactics and special operations. They also assist other U.S. and allied forces and agencies, plan and conduct unilateral SF operations, and perform other special operations as directed. The detachment serves as a manpower pool from which SF commanders organize tailored SF teams to perform specific missions. In addition to the skills of operations and intelligence, communications, medical aid, engineering, and weapons, each Special Forces soldier is taught to train, advise, and assist host nation military or paramilitary forces.

Special Forces soldiers are highly skilled operators, trainers, and teachers. Area oriented, these soldiers are specially trained in their area's native language and culture.

A view of an AN/PRC-126 radio, which is used primarily for internal communications among SF team members in the field.

Used as an emergency beacon, this AN/PRC-112 radio emits a signal on an emergency frequency that allows SF soldiers to be located anywhere.

RADIO SET, AN/PRC-112
PART NO. 01-P21261J001
NSN: 5820-01-279-5450
MFR: 94990 SER. NO.
CONTRACT: DAAB07-90-C-H025
US

The AN/PRC-119 is a frequency jumping secure radio primarily used by U.S. Army ground forces.

This keyboard is used by the Special Forces to send and receive typed in, encrypted, data messages over a radio frequency. When coupled with a radio, it keeps signals from being effectively monitored by enemy forces even when used behind enemy lines.

In general, A-teams are equipped with communications, as in tactical satellite communications, high-frequency radios, and global positioning systems. Medical kits include laboratory and dental instruments and supplies, sterilizer, resuscitator, aspirator, water-testing kits, and veterinary equipment. Other key equipment includes individual and perimeter defense weapons, as well as electric and nonelectric demolitions and night vision devices. Specialized equipment can be added for specific missions. For underwater or waterborne infiltration, scuba teams are equipped with open-circuit twin 80s scuba tanks, Zodiac boat, and Klepper kayaks. Military free-fall parachuting teams use ram-air parachutes and oxygen systems for high-altitude, low-opening parachuting.

Special Forces soldiers are carefully selected, specially trained, and capable of extended operations in extremely remote and hostile territory. They train to perform given doctrinal missions: foreign internal defense, unconventional warfare, special reconnaissance, direct action, and counterterrorism. While Special Forces soldiers are capable of performing all of these missions, an increasing emphasis is being placed on foreign internal defense and coalition warfare and support. FID operations are designed to help friendly developing nations by working with host country military and police forces to improve their technical skills, understanding of human rights issues and to help with humanitarian and civic action projects.

A new mission that has emerged as a result of Operation Desert Storm is coalition warfare and support. Coalition warfare and support draws on the Special Forces soldier's maturity, military skills, language skills, and cultural awareness. It ensures the ability of a wide variety of foreign troops to work together effectively in a wide range of military exercises or operations such as Operation Desert Storm.

MISSIONS

In the 1980s, Special Forces missions were re-emphasized, and the number of units began to grow again with the reactivation of the 1st and 3rd Special Forces Groups. The Department of the Army also created a separate Army branch for Special Forces soldiers and officers on April 19, 1987. Special Forces soldiers were once again called on to train other nations' soldiers in fighting communist guerrillas, but this time in Central America, and most notably, El Salvador. Their actions and training helped the Salvadorian forces defeat insurgents and eliminated the possible need for direct conventional U.S. force involvement.

In December 1989, Special Forces soldiers from 7th Special Forces Group were the initial forces for Operation Just Cause in Panama. Their actions in defeating the Panamanian Defense Force soldiers at the Pacora River Bridge stopped the reinforcement of the Tocumen/Torrijo Airport, where the 82nd Airborne Division was attacking. The soldiers of the 7th also disabled television transmission towers, stifling the announcement of the American invasion to PDF units. Because of their Spanish-speaking abilities and their intimate knowledge of the geography, society, and military of the country, 7th SFG teams spread

During a modular demonstration, a mannequin is dressed to resemble a High Altitude Low Opening (HALO) and High Altitude High Opening (HAHO) parachutist. He is dressed in a black jumpsuit with an MC-4 parachute, oxygen mask, helmet, and an M41A Carbine.

87

The AN/PRC-137 radio is a high-frequency, long-range communications radio with an integrated security system. This state-of-the-art radio provides the Special Forces communications sergeant with general purpose message traffic.

This small solar panel is a Special Operations power source. It gives the Special Forces communications sergeant the ability to recharge radio batteries, even in a hostile environment.

The STG77, chambered for 5.56x.45 mm NATO round, is made in Austria.

The following weapons are all made in Germany by Heckler and Koch (from top to bottom): the MG3 machine gun, the G3AR rifle, the P-7 semiautomatic 9 mm pistol, and the MP5A3 9 mm submachine gun.

A Makarov semi automatic pistol, chambered for a 9x18 mm round, is made in Russia.

The Heckler and Koch Universal Self-Loading Pistol (USP), a .45 ACP. This is the civilian model of the new Special Operations Forces sidearm, made in Germany.

Top: A Russian-made AK-47.
Bottom: A French-manufactured FAMAS.

Some of the U.S. Army Special Operations weapons (from top to bottom): a U.S.–made M-16 with an M203 40 mm grenade launcher, an M9 semi-automatic 9 mm pistol, and an M4A1 carbine that is semiautomatic and fully automatic and equipped with an Advanced Combat Optical Gunsight. The latter weapon is widely used by Special Operations Forces.

Weapons that Special Forces soldiers in the Russian theater of operations might be expected to find include (from top to bottom): a DshK 108 mm machine gun, an SG43 machine gun, a Druganov rifle, and an AGS-17 30 mm grenade launcher.

A set of PVS-7 Night Vision Goggles with headset. As night vision is essential to the any soldier working under the cover of darkness, this device provides Special Forces soldiers the ability to see at night under even the darkest conditions.

This pack is a Multi-Purpose Special Operations Antenna Kit, which gives the Special Forces communications sergeant the ability to communicate with higher command from great distances.

A buoyancy compensator and regulator lay on top of a pair of Twin 80s SCUBA tanks. The twin tanks allow a swimmer to stay submerged for a longer period of time and allow for him to approach a target from a greater distance.

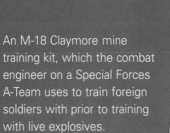

An M-18 Claymore mine training kit, which the combat engineer on a Special Forces A-Team uses to train foreign soldiers with prior to training with live explosives.

throughout the country over the next several days to persuade isolated garrisons and communities to accept defeat. They also acted as guides to U.S. conventional forces. Once Panamanian strongman Manuel Noreiga was captured and the legitimate government of Panama was in place, 7th SFG soldiers shifted gears and helped train the new Panamanian army.

The need for Special Forces soldiers' skills continued to grow in the 1990s. As a result, the 1st Special Operations Command was renamed the U.S. Army Special Forces Command (Airborne) and headquartered at Fort Bragg under a major command, the U.S. Army Special Operations Command. In 1991, 5th Special Forces Group, and later 3rd and part of 10th Groups, deployed to Saudi Arabia as part of the U.S. forces for Operation Desert Shield. Their main task was to train and advise the Arab Coalition forces, including the Kuwaiti resistance. When offensive operations began, Special Forces soldiers conducted special reconnaissance mis-

An MX-122 Remote Firing device, which is used by Special Forces engineers to detonate explosives from a safe distance away from the target area. It consists of a radio transmitter and ten receivers.

While receiving a message from another soldier, a Special Forces student watches for enemy forces near a command post set up by their squad in the woods. His weapon is a M16A2 rifle.

A group of students huddle with a group of simulated guerrillas as they plan a strategy with a terrain map of the area. The exercise requires an SF group to meet up with and train a band of guerrilla soldiers and accomplish a battle objective.

A Special Forces student and a simulated guerrilla soldier plan their troop's movements during the Robin Sage exercise. In their unique role as teachers in the special operations community, Special Forces soldiers must perfect their leadership and teaching skills so that they can effectively communicate methods and ideas to the soldiers of allied forces.

Keeping watch on a command post set up by their squad in the woods of North Carolina, a Special Forces student watches for enemy forces which are part of the Robin Sage exercise, one of the most realistic-type final exams any soldier can go through. The vastness of the North Carolina countryside and extensive wooded areas provide an excellent training area.

sions into Iraq and Kuwait. Many of these missions sent teams hundreds of miles into the enemy's areas, where they reported on Iraqi activities. These Intelligence reports helped the coalition forces prepare the ground campaign, which led to the defeat of the Iraqi army and the liberation of Kuwait.

After Desert Storm, Gen. H. Norman Schwarzkopf, the commander of the coalition forces, described Special Forces soldiers as the "eyes and ears" of conventional forces and as the "glue that held coalition forces together." As Operation Desert Storm began to wind down, the Kurds of Northern Iraq and other indigenous tribes rebelled against a weakened Iraqi president Saddam Hussein. The Kurds were driven from their villages and forced into the mountains along the Turkish-Iraqi border, where an average of 450 died each day. Soldiers from 10th Special Forces Group deployed to the area and began to conduct humanitarian relief operations for more than half a million Kurdish refugees. The Special Forces soldiers provided emergency relief and basic services and eventually moved the refugees to resettlement camps. Operation Provide Comfort showed the world that

A Special Forces squad leader looks to an instructor for advice on a scenario during the Robin Sage exercise, the final exam for SF trainees. Instructors won't readily hand out advice, as students are expected to work out their own problems as they would have to do in a real-life situation.

Special Forces has the organization and capability to conduct large-scale relief operations immediately following a major conflict such as Desert Storm.

In September 1994, 3rd Special Forces Group deployed to the Caribbean nation of Haiti to ensure a peaceful transition from a repressive totalitarian government to a democratically elected one. In less than two months, its soldiers controlled almost 95 percent of the land mass and roughly 65 percent of the population. As the conditions in Haiti improved, 3rd Group was withdrawn and replaced by Special Forces teams from the National Guard's 19th and 20th Special Forces Groups.

As the United States found itself maintaining peace in Bosnia, Special Forces soldiers found themselves at the lead. The 10th Special Forces Group deployed troops to act as liaisons between the U.S. forces and the other forces making up a multinational force there. Special Forces soldiers also taught mine-clearing techniques to help remove the thousands of mines scattered throughout the countryside.

Special Forces soldiers continue to serve at home and abroad, providing humanitarian aid and assisting with foreign internal defense in friendly foreign nations. They continue willingly to undertake difficult missions in order to help those who are less fortunate. Special Forces men are quiet professionals, living by their motto "De Oppresso Liber"- To Free the Oppressed.

A Special Forces communications sergeant works with a mobile radio during the Cabanas '97 exercise held in Panama, which brought together U.S. Special Forces teams with soldiers from four Central American countries.

Teaching tactics to soldiers from four Central American countries, a Special Forces soldier in Panama on the U.S. base at Fort Sherman, uses his skills as a teacher and a soldier to explain a combat maneuver in their native Spanish.

Two standard U.S. Army pistols are (from top to bottom) the M1911A1 semi-automatic 45 ACP pistol, and the M9 semiautomatic 9-mm pistol.

RIGHT
Soldiers from the U.S. Army 10th Special Forces Group and Russian soldiers on joint patrol during Operation Joint Endeavor in Bosnia-Hercegovina examine abandoned military equipment and hardware. *U.S. Army Photo*

CHAPTER FOUR

U. S. AIR FORCE
SPECIAL
OPERATIONS

They don't fly jets. Many of them spend more time with Army and Navy personnel than their Air Force counterparts. And some are trained like SEALs or Green Berets, and know very little about airplanes or helicopters. They are the members of the Air Force Special Operations Command (AFSOC), which operates at four major bases around the world, but is based at out-of-the-way Hurlburt Field in the Florida panhandle. While most people don't think about the Air Force when the subject is Special Operations missions, AFSOC members fulfill one of the most vital roles. Without Air Force special operators, members of the Rangers, Marine Force Recon, Delta, SEALs, and Green Berets would have a tough time infiltrating enemy lines, getting resupplied, receiving quick fire support, or being rescued.

HISTORY

At the height of World War II, in August 1943, the Army Air Forces formed Project 9, America's first air commando unit, and the precursor to today's Air Force Special Operations units. Later called the 5318th Provisional Unit (Air), the unit flew supply and intelligence missions for Wingate's Raiders, a British commando unit on the ground in Japanese-occupied Burma.

Meanwhile, in Europe, air commandos working closely with the Office of Strategic Services (OSS), a group of flyers code-named Carpetbaggers, were flying secret nighttime missions behind enemy lines to supply resistance fighters and deliver Jedburgh teams—the predecessors of today's Special Forces. Flying surplus B-24 bombers that had been painted black to help avoid detection, the Carpetbaggers flew just 300 feet to 400 feet above the ground so as not to be spotted by radar. Although the air commandos—which also included a unit that operated in

An ominous sight by any means, the Air Force MH-53J Pave Low III Helicopter is a multi-million dollar aircraft that boasts some of the most advanced navigational equipment in the world. Its terrain-following, terrain-avoidance radar, forward-looking infrared sensor, and Doppler navigation systems, along with a projected map display, enable the crew to follow terrain contours and avoid obstacles, making low-level penetration possible.

An Air Force MC-130H Combat Talon II, of the 16th Special Operations Wing, 15th Special Operations Squadron, shows off its countermeasure flare release capability as it flies off the coast of Florida.

Southern Europe—were successful in helping to turn the tide of World War II, the units were disbanded at the end of the war as the U.S. military began its postwar downsizing.

Though the U.S. forces flew limited Special Operations missions during the Korean War—often in concert with the Central Intelligence Agency—it was not until 1961 that air commandos would become an institutionalized part of the Air Force. In April 1961, Air Force Chief of Staff General Curtis LeMay created the 4400th Combat Crew Training Squadron on an underused portion of Eglin Air Force Base in the Florida panhandle to support Army counter-insurgency units. (That section of Eglin is now Hurlburt Field.) Almost immediately, the air commandos began operating in Laos as part of Operation Mill Pond, flying reconnaissance missions and making bombing runs. Because the air crews were supposed to be operating only as advisors, the commandos worked closely with the CIA. Identifying markings on their planes were removed and the pilots wore civilian clothes and operated under assumed identities. By November 1961, the crews were conducting missions in Vietnam. One of the more controversial aspects of Air Force Special Operations units in Vietnam was called Operation Ranch Hand, the spraying of herbicide—including Agent Orange—on wide swaths of the countryside. Though the defoliants did clear large portions of jungle growth, which enemy troops used to conceal themselves, the chemicals have been linked to illnesses among U.S. servicemen and the Vietnamese who came in contact with Agent Orange.

Air commandos also flew combat and supply missions, propaganda runs in which they broadcast messages via bullhorns,

A KC-135 aircraft from the Air Mobility Command refuels an Air Force MC-130E Combat Talon I of the 8th Special Operations Squadron off the coast of Florida during a daylight refueling mission. The MC-130E, when fueled, can also act as a refueling platform for other aircraft if needed.

The rear gunner aboard an Air Force MH-53J Pave Low III helicopter takes aim on a target during a training mission over ranges at Hurlburt Field in Florida. The MH-53J is considered one of the most advanced helicopters in the world, and was the aircraft that led the charge of Apache helicopters during the initial assault of the Gulf War.

An Air Force MH-53J Pave Low III helicopter warms up before takeoff at Hurlburt Field in Florida. The MH-53J is one of the most powerful, technologically advanced helicopters in the military's inventory. It has a maximum speed of 165 miles per hour, a crew of six, range of 550 nautical miles, aerial refueling capability, and can carry up to 38 troops or 14 litters.

and rescue operations. The most famous of the rescue missions is the Son Tay raid, launched in 1970 to free U.S. servicemen believed to be held in a prisoner of war camp near Hanoi. Though the mission failed to turn up any POWs, the operation showed that the Air Force was able to conduct high-risk missions deep into hostile territory without taking casualties.

Ten years later however, by the time of the Operation Rice Bowl hostage rescue mission in Iran, the Air Force had lost its capability to conduct such operations. As a result, the rescue force consisted largely of Navy RH-53D Sea Stallion helicopters flown by pilots from the Air Force and Marine Corps. The ill-fated rescue ended when one of the helicopters collided with one of the C-130 transport planes at the Desert One refueling site. Eight soldiers were killed, five were injured, wreckage littered Iranian desert, and Special Operations suffered a major black eye. After the Desert One disaster, the Air Force paid more attention to its Special Operations side and as a result, the first Pave Lows were developed.

During the Grenada invasion in 1983 and later, during Operation Just Cause in Panama in 1989, Air Force commandos rebounded, and despite several communications snafus between gunships and SEALs and Rangers on the ground, the high-tech AC-130 Spectre gunship and Pave Lows solidified their reputations as life-savers for Army and Navy special operators.

SELECTION AND TRAINING
AFSOC training has among the highest dropout rate of any Special Operations group in the U.S. military. More than 70 percent of those who try out do not make it. The result is that the expanding AFSOC command is plagued by shortages, particularly for pararescue personnel, also called PJs, and combat controllers.

Two Air Force MH-60G Pave Hawk helicopters take off in formation during a training flight over the Gulf Coast. The MH-60G's primary wartime missions are infiltration, exfiltration, resupply of Special Operations Forces during day, night, or marginal weather conditions, and search and rescue operations.

Members of the Air Force's 23rd Special Tactics Squadron climb up towards two hovering Air Force helicopters as they practice one of their quick extraction techniques. The ability to get in and out of an area quickly is often the basis for a successful mission.

PJs and combat controllers, grouped together as special tactics forces, undergo year-long training regimens that are as tough on the body and as taxing on the mind as any in the military. Seventy-seven percent who try to make the special tactics teams do not. To become a PJ or combat controller, candidates start by attending 10 weeks at Pararescue/Combat Control Pre-Conditioning School at Lackland Air Force Base near San Antonio, Texas. Next, they move on to four weeks at Special Forces Combat Diver School at Key West Naval Air Station in Florida, followed by the three week U.S. Army Basic Airborne School at Fort Benning, Georgia. Afterward, for four weeks, they learn advanced parachuting techniques at the Army's Freefall School at Fort Bragg, North Carolina, and spend 17 days at the Air Force's Combat Survival School at Fairchild Air Force Base near Spokane, Washington. Then, the exhausted candidates train for a one-day course in underwater egress training.

The PJ trainees move on to 32 weeks of pararescue training at Kirtland Air Force Base in Albuquerque, New Mexico, where they are taught combat medical skills. Combat control trainees go to the Air Traffic Control School at Keesler Air Force Base in Biloxi, Mississippi, for 16 weeks, and then spend another 13 weeks at the Combat Control School at Pope Air Force Base, North Carolina. Pilots of AFSOC's air assets train at Kirtland Air Base, where their low-level training runs in the sparsely populated deserts and mountains of New Mexico disturb almost no one. Most of those selected as AFSOC pilots have already flown Army or Air Force craft.

Training for the Pave Low—the most sophisticated of the aircraft—takes about eight months and focuses mostly on brains, not brawn. The Pave Low is so complicated that to operate the helicopter requires a pilot, a copilot, and a flight engineer to interpret and monitor all the various navigation

systems. Three crew members in the back must lean out of the side and back hatches to visually monitor what is outside and relay that information to the pilot.

ORGANIZATION

Since the 1st Special Operations Wing at Hurlburt Field was nearly transferred to the Army in 1984, the Air Force's special operators have come a long way. Though they are in perennial battles with the fighter pilot side of the service for money and attention, they have had their own command since 1990.

The Air Force Special Operations Command (AFSOC) is the Air Force's contribution to the U.S. Special Operations Command, which also oversees the Rangers, SEALs, Green Berets, and other units. AFSOC is based at Hurlburt Field, Florida, and is divided into several components. The command consists of about 13,000 active duty and reserve troops and about 102 fixed wing aircraft and 58 rotary wing aircraft. The Air Force Special Operations School trains U.S. and allied personnel in special operations and regional cultures and politics.

The major active duty AFSOC groups are the 16th Special Operations Wing, based at Hurlburt Field, and charged with missions in North and South America and the Middle East; the 352nd Special Operations Group at Royal Air Force Base, Mindenhall, United Kingdom, tasked with Europe and Africa; and the 353rd Special Operations Group at Kadena Air Base in Japan, which is tasked with Asia and the Pacific. The 18th Flight Test Squadron, based at Hurlburt, tests Special Operations aircraft and equipment. The 720th Special Tactics Group is charged with combat control and pararescue operations. Special Operations combat controllers and pararescue personnel work jointly in special tac-

TOP LEFT

An Air Force gunner inspects a 105-mm gun, part of the weapons systems aboard an AC-130H Spectre Gunship, while performing a portion of the aircraft's preflight checklist as they prepare to deploy from Hurlburt Field. Debuting in Vietnam in 1972, gunships like these destroyed more than 10,000 enemy trucks and were credited with many life-saving close air support missions. During Operation Urgent Fury in Grenada, these heavily armed aircraft suppressed enemy air defense systems and directly attacked ground forces. They have also played key roles in Operation Just Cause in Panama, Operation Desert Storm, and operations in Somalia and Bosnia.

An Air Force flight crew aboard an AC-130H Spectre Gunship from the 16th Special Operations Wing begins the aircraft's preflight checklist as they prepare to deploy from Hurlburt Field. The aircraft has a range of 1,300 nautical miles, aerial refueling capability, three main guns, and crew of 14.

LEFT

An Air Force fire control officer aboard an AC-130H Spectre Gunship begins the aircraft's preflight checklist as they prepare to deploy from Hurlburt Field.

An Air Force STS team member sets up his line of fire around a Florida training area. Special Tactics Squadrons consist of combat controllers and pararescue personnel who deploy by air, sea, and land into hostile areas.

Providing cover for his team members, an Air Force STS team member takes up a kneeling position ready to engage any potential threat as his team plots their next move during a training mission.

An Air Force Pararescue soldier prepares a simulated trauma patient for helicopter evacuation out of a forward area during a training mission in Florida. As part of Special Tactics Teams working alongside combat controllers, pararescue personnel deploy by air, sea, and land into forward, nonpermissive environments and provide the trauma medical care necessary to stabilize and evacuate injured personnel.

tics teams. Combat controllers are responsible for air traffic control, establishing landing zones, and calling for close air support, while PJs set up aid stations and care for the injured.

AFSOC is also responsible for an Air National Guard unit, the 193rd Special Operations Wing based at Harrisburg International Airport in Pennsylvania, and an Air Force Reserve unit, the 919th Special Operations Wing based at Duke Field, Florida.

EQUIPMENT

The U.S. has the best-equipped air force in the world, and its special operators have aircraft so sophisticated that their interiors resemble something out of a futuristic fantasy. The $40 million MH-53J Pave Low is particularly advanced. Unlike conventional helicopters, the Pave Low comes equipped with forward-looking infrared radar (FLIR), terrain avoidance and following radar and radar jammers. This enables a pilot to fly at less than 100 feet above the ground, at night, without being detected, and to arrive exactly on target. The navigation system on the chopper, which carries a crew of six, is the most sophisticated in the world—and it can fly 600 miles without refueling.

The MH-60G Pave Hawk is primarily used for carrying Army and Navy special operators deep behind enemy lines and can carry up to 10 troops. The MC-130 E/H Combat Talon I and II transports and MC-130P Combat Shadows are used primarily for airborne drops and refueling Special Operations helicopters. The EC-130E Commando Solo flown by the 193rd Special Operations Wing in Pennsylvania, is used for psychological operation missions, including propaganda broadcasts. The plane can receive, transmit, and ana-

Refueling behind an MC-130E Combat Talon I, are two MH-60G Pave Hawk helicopters. Both are part of the 16th Special Operations Wing.

An Air Force MH-53J Pave Low III Helicopter from the 20th Special Operations Squadron based at Hurlburt Field, Florida, fires countermeasure flares into the skies. MH-53J's were used in a variety of missions during Desert Storm, and were among the first aircraft into Iraq when they led Army AH-64 Apaches to destroy Iraqi early warning radars. In addition to infiltration, exfiltration, and resupply of special forces teams throughout Iraq and Kuwait, Pave Lows provided search and rescue coverage for coalition air forces throughout the region.

An Air Force AC-130U "Spooky" gunship from the 16th Special Operations Wing, 4th Special Operations Squadron. The aircraft has three sizes of mounted guns and can strike a target with pinpoint accuracy from altitudes of 18,000 feet.

lyze a variety of different electronic signals, and also has jamming and deception capabilities.

AFSOC's signature aircraft is probably the AC-130 gunship, which travels at speeds up to 300 miles per hour, and has a FLIR system that can deliniate enemy from friendly soldiers. These ultramodern planes can handle a variety of missions, but they are best known for their close air support and precision firing. The AC-130H Spectre is the basic model and was the plane that destroyed the Panamanian Defense Force headquarters.

The newer AC-130U gunship is even better. It can fly higher, allows the 13-member crew to see better, and its weapons can be fired with even greater precision. The $72 million plane is equipped with a computer-guided fire-control system that allows the planes to engage two targets simultaneously. It is a virtual artillery battery. Its 25-mm Gatling gun fires 1,800 rounds per minute. Its 40-mm cannon can fire 100 shots each minute. And its huge 105-mm Howitzer fires 6 to 10 rounds each minute. The aircraft also has low-light level television (LLLTV), which uses ambient light to provide a black-and-white image of the ground below, as well as several radio systems. Because nearly all missions are flown at night, the pilots and crews of the planes wear the most modern night vision goggles (NVG) in the world. The $6,000 goggles allow air crews to pick out terrain features even when the moon is not full.

MISSIONS

The missions of Air Force special operators include conducting unconventional warfare, special reconnaissance, humanitarian assistance, psychological operations, counternarcotics, direct action, personnel recovery, and foreign internal defense. Air Force commandos were particularly busy during Operation Desert Storm. A Pave Low crew rescued an F-14 fighter pilot shot down in Iraq. Other Pave Low crews ferried Army Special Forces members deep into Iraq on special reconnaissance missions and led U.S. Army AH-64 Apaches on an operation to destroy Iraqi radar installations that started the air war. But Air Force special operators also suffered the largest single loss of the air war when an AC-130H Spectre gunship was shot down by an Iraqi

MC-130H Combat Talon II attached to the 8th Special Operations Squadron flies over the water off the coast of Florida.

Unlike the H model, the AC-130U has dual target attack capability (the ability to attack two targets simultaneously) and engage a target in zero visibility through use of a radar weapons system modified from that on the F-15 Strike Eagle.

Crew members of an Air Force C-130 transport stand at the rear of the aircraft as they lower the back ramp of the plane after landing. This plain version of a C-130 offers support, and is attached to the 16th Special Operations Wing based at Hurlburt Field, Florida. The aircraft can carry everything from troops to vehicles.

An Air Force AC-130H Spectre Gunship from the 16th Special Operations Wing, 16th Special Operations Squadron, based at Hurlburt Field, Florida. The aircraft's primary missions are close air support, air interdiction, and armed reconnaissance. The aircraft is equipped with radar and electronic sensors that give the gunship a method of positively identifying friendly ground forces.

The patch on a flight suit that indicates the person is a member of U.S. Air Force Special Operations community. They are some of the best trained aviators and soldiers in the world, and fly and possess some of the most technologically superior aircraft and weapons that exist today.

SA-16 surface-to-air missile. The 1st Special Operations Wing aircraft was carrying 14 crew members. All died. The plane had been helping to repel an Iraqi attack on a U.S. Marine outpost at the Saudi Arabian border town of Khafji.

More recently, air commandos have been among the most active force in the U.S. military. In 1995, AC-130H Spectre gunships knocked out Serbian artillery sites around Sarajevo in Bosnia-Herzegovina, and special operators also evacuated Americans from the U.S. Embassy compound in Liberia in 1996. They set up an airfield for humanitarian aid in Rwanda in 1994, and helped rescue stranded Rangers in Somalia in 1992. Air commandos have also helped to enforce the no-fly zone in Iraq since the end of Desert Storm, and trained various forces of other nations around the globe.

CHAPTER FIVE U.S.
MARINE FORCE RECONNAISSANCE

Though much of the public has never heard of these guys, Marine Force Reconnaissance units have been around since World War II. By the 1960s, Force Recon was so proficient at special operations that its commanders were hesitant to go on exercises with the newly formed Navy SEALs because the Marines believed the SEALs' training level was inadequate.

Force Recon has continued its tradition of intense training, as well as its usually friendly rivalry with the SEALs. They sometimes miss out on high-profile missions and the glamour that comes with them, because, in part, the U.S. Marine Corps is not a member of the U.S. Special Operations Command, which includes the SEALs, Rangers, and Green Berets. But Force Recon members are trained to do most of what the other Special Operations Forces can do—and some they cannot. As is true with SEALs, they conduct amphibious missions and ship and oil platform takedowns. Similar to the Rangers, they often fight in small units, are airborne qualified, and train under a variety of climates. And like Special Forces and Delta, their mission statement includes conducting special reconnaissance and counterterrorism operations.

SELECTION AND TRAINING

The training of a Force Recon Marine is among the most intense—and longest—in the military. Candidates must have three to five years of excellent performance in the Corps and must have the rank of corporal. The first hurdle in selection is the one when most of the trainees wash out. First, candidates must pass a physical screening test, which is immediately followed by a PT test. The PT test includes a timed three-mile run, pullups, sit-ups, and completing an obstacle course—twice. From there, they move to the swimming pool, where they jump in wearing their uniforms, including boots, and swim 500 yards in 17 minutes.

A Force Recon unit holds its position in an area of bushes and shrubs that provides good cover from any opposing force. Because history has shown that the major portion of a battle often begins when the Marines have come ashore, these Marines precede their main force by days or even weeks. They can be sent in for intelligence purposes, to disable a specific target, or aid their Special Operations counterparts.

Individual members of two teams of the U.S. Marines 1st Force Reconnaissance unit move into the open ocean off Camp Pendleton in California at dusk for a night insertion training exercise. While not deployed, teams will constantly practice and perform their skills and tactics by simulating missions and other situations for which they might be called upon.

Members of the U.S. Marines 1st Force Reconnaissance Unit parachute into a training area at Camp Pendleton, California. The Force Recon Marines, like many Special Operations teams, are trained to enter into an area from all possible means, by land, sea, or air, and thus are extensively trained in all these areas.

They are then required to tread water for one minute carrying their M16s. With little or no rest, they put on 50-pound rucksacks and go on a 2 1/2-hour march. They are then given a written exam to test their professional competence, and finally, are interviewed by Force Recon veterans who make the final determination whether the candidate has the right stuff.

The selection exams are given once a month, and only three or four of the 15 or 20 who try out are actually selected to train. Once selected however, most of the dropouts fail to complete the course because they are injured. Those who make the cut move on to the Force Reconnaissance Individual Training Phase for six months to learn basic and advanced skills. In addition to learning patrolling techniques and other infantry tactics, the candidates complete the Army's airborne course; the Combatant Diving School, where they learn open and closed-circuit breathing systems; and the Survival Evasion Resistance Escape (SERE) school.

At Force Recon's advanced training school, candidates attend an eight-week version of the U.S. Army Ranger course; the Army's Mountain Leaders Course, where they learn winter survival and rock climbing; Pathfinder School; and receive training in free-fall parachuting, shooting, and basic medical skills. Next, the candidates go through the Unit Training Phase for six months. The seven training packages are long-range communications, including satellite communication (SATCOM), Morse code, and multiband radios;

Marine Gunnery Sgt. Bob Gray readies to enter the water on a training mission at USMC base Camp Pendleton in California using the LAR V Draeger rebreather. This diving apparatus has become standard equipment throughout the Special Operations community because of its ability to allow the "rebreathing" of a diver's expelled air.

amphibious training, including learning how to conduct hydrographic surveys and launching from submarines and other vessels; arms training, where they learn how to call for close air support; an advanced dive course, where they fine-tune infiltration and extraction techniques; advanced parachuting, including high altitude, high opening (HAHO) into unlit drop zones from 25,000 feet; and foreign weapons training, where they are trained to identify and fire weapons from other countries. Along the way, they conduct several live-fire exercises, including one in an urban environment, and are trained in demolitions.

The finale is a field exercise in which they combine everything they have learned. The exercise includes amphibious infiltrations and extractions, a parachute jump, hydrographic surveys, and mountain and desert patrols at bases around the United States. Afterward, the candidates are assigned to one of the MEUs stationed around the world for another six months. The focus is training for direct action missions, which include hostage rescues, helicopter deployments, and takedowns of ships and oil platforms. Before they are Special Operations certified (SOC), the platoon must successfully pass its assigned portion of a field exercise that encompasses everything they have learned. Finally, they are deployed for six months, usually to the Persian Gulf. Marines usually spend about five years in Force Recon units.

ORGANIZATION

The basic Force Recon unit is a team of three to five men, led by a staff sergeant, including two scouts and a radio operator. Four or five teams make up each platoon, which is led by a captain and made up of 20 men, including a U.S. Navy corpsman. Six platoons make up a company, commanded by a lieutenant colonel. Each company includes a

Members of the 1st Force Reconnaissance unit of the U.S. Marine Corps train to advance onto the beach at Camp Pendleton, from the water. These members, new to the unit, practice for the first few times without weapons and other equipment, so they can first concentrate more on procedure and technique. Actual missions would take place under the cover of darkness, the time at which most Special Operations teams prefer to work for obvious tactical advantages.

TOP RIGHT
Two teams of U.S. Marines 1st Force Reconnaissance unit members move into the open ocean off Camp Pendleton in California at dusk for a night insertion training exercise. Although the Marines are mostly known for their ground operations, these Special Operations units are extensively trained for the water environment.

RIGHT
Force Recon members ready their equipment for a static line jump into a training area as part of a night insertion mission. For this group, it will be their last jump before deploying.

headquarters platoon with intelligence, communications, and supply sections.

The 1st Force Reconnaissance Company, based at Camp Pendleton, California, is responsible for the Persian Gulf and the Pacific Ocean area. The 2nd Recon Company, based at Camp Lejeune, North Carolina, is responsible for the Mediterranean Sea area; and the 5th Recon Company is based at Okinawa, Japan, and is tasked with Asia. The 1st and 2nd companies each have five platoons, while the 5th has three platoons.

EQUIPMENT

The basic squad weapon is the M-16, but Force Recon members are also armed with MP5 submachine guns and shotguns, depending on the mission. On amphibious operations, they use SCUBA or LAR V Draeger closed-circuit breathing devises and deploy from Combat Rubber Raiding Craft (CRRC), submarines, and destroyers.

MISSIONS

Force Recon members conduct amphibious and deep ground reconnaissance, surveillance, and recovery of sensitive materials. They also perform hostage rescues, raids and participate in unconventional warfare in support of Marine Expeditionary Forces, and task forces, including joint operations with other Special Operations units.

RIGHT
Lt. Col. Jim Thomas, a member of the U.S. Marines 1st Force Reconnaissance Unit, parachutes toward earth after a team training jump at Camp Pendleton, California.

Force Recon members ready their equipment for a static line jump into a training area as part of a night insertion mission. For this group, this will be their last jump before deploying.

A Force Recon member adjusts his LAR V Draeger rebreather before entering the open ocean for a training exercise. The LAR V Draeger is a self-contained, closed-circuit, 100 percent oxygen, underwater breathing apparatus designed for clandestine operations in shallow water. With this closed circuit system, the diver breathes 100 percent oxygen, and his exhaled breath is passed through a chemical filter that removes carbon dioxide, replenishing the oxygen that is consumed. Depth, water temperature, and oxygen consumption rate all affect the duration of the LAR V Draeger.

The road to the formation of a Marine Corps special reconnaissance unit started in the 1920s, when Maj. Earl H. Ellis began a study of the Pacific Islands, including Japan. He noted economic vitality, potential enemy capabilities as well as climate, topography, population, and sea conditions. He also included a strategy for how the United States might capture important islands for air bases in the event of a U.S.–Japanese war. When that war did come, 20 years later, many of his studies were consulted and some of his strategies were used.

The first Marine Corps unit formed specifically to conduct amphibious reconnaissance started in 1942 at Quantico, Virginia. The new unit, called Observer Group, was composed of two officers and 20 enlisted men.

However, their mission, which was to prepare for an invasion of North Africa, was scrapped. By 1943, the unit had been rechristened the Amphibious Reconnaissance Company and boarded a submarine headed for the Pacific. The target, Apanama Atoll, was deemed important because it was suitable for a sea base. After midnight, on November 20, the recon team paddled across the island's

Waiting for the command to begin approaching a fortified building during a simulated hostage rescue operation, a Force Recon marine at Camp Pendleton reviews in his mind the objective and waits from cover to begin his squad's approach.

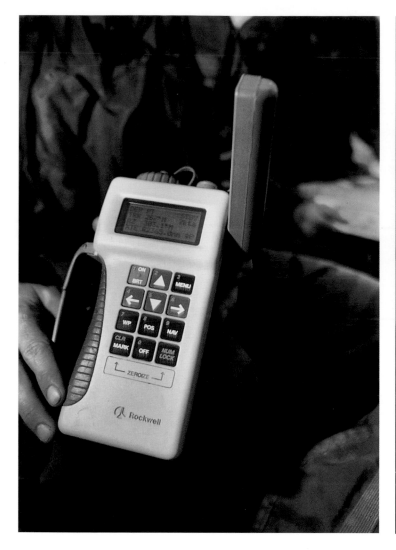

Using a waterproof, hand-held global positioning system (GPS) like this, Marines and other Special Operations units can accurately pinpoint their location and distance to their objective within approximately 50 feet at any given time. Although not used as their sole source of navigation, equipment such as this serves as a strong backup and acts as a quick reference for calculations formerly done in longhand.

An individual member of two teams of the U.S. Marines 1st Force Reconnaissance unit move into the open ocean off Camp Pendleton in California at dusk for a night insertion training exercise. While not deployed, teams will constantly practice and perform their skills and tactics by simulating missions and other situations for which they might be called upon.

coral reef prepared to collect information about the Japanese forces on the island. As they advanced toward the enemy position, they were taken under fire, and a battle ensued. One Marine was killed, but the recon team was able to capture the island, clearing the way for a larger Marine landing. After several more successful efforts on neighboring islands, the recon company was expanded into a battalion of 20 officers, 270 enlisted men, and 13 Navy medics. The new Amphibious Recon Battalion scouted beaches at Tinian prior to the Allied landing, and participated in the battles for Iwo Jima, in February 1945, and Okinawa the following month.

A second Marine Corps recon unit, called Special Services Unit Number 1, was also active during the war in the Southwest Pacific. In addition to Marines, the special unit included Australians, as well as partisans from the Japanese-occupied islands of New Guinea and New Britain. Prior to any Allied landing, the Special Services Unit would

first conduct reconnaissance, often in native canoes or through thick jungles. Information provided included sketches and pictures of terrain, as well as reports on the size of enemy forces, which helped the Allies determine when and how to attack.

During the Korean War, recon Marines conducted missions with Navy Underwater Demolition Teams (UDTs). On several occasions, the joint teams penetrated deep into North Korea to destroy bridges and tunnels. But as the Allied war effort stalled, Marine Recon units were limited to short-range patrols and assignments guarding military bases.

After the Korean War, Marine recon marines were sent to the Army's airborne school at Fort Benning, Georgia, and by 1958, the Corps had formed two modern reconnaissance teams. The mission of the First and Second Force Re-connaissance companies was to provide long-range reconnaissance up to 100 miles inland. Each of the companies was composed of teams that specialized in amphibious recon, parachute

sailors needed as long as 18 months to become SEALs, while Marines could arrive at the same proficiency in six months. The performance of SEALs in Vietnam changed many Marine Corps minds, but the rivalry between Force Recon and the SEALs continues today.

During the Cuban missle crisis in 1962, a recon platoon from the First Force Company prepared to take part in the possible invasion of Cuba. The mission, called OPLAN 314, was called off when the Soviet Union backed down and began removing missles from Cuba.

The war in Vietnam was as frustrating for Force Recon as it was for the rest of American troops. They were misused by the Marine Corps hierarchy, the intelligence they collected was often ignored, and their presence, as "an elite within an elite" (the Marine Corps was viewed as already being elite), offended many in the egalitarian minded Corps. Further, Force Recon members were taken away from their regular units to work for the CIA's secret Studies and Observation Group (SOG), which was essentially fighting a parallel war in Vietnam. The SOG, the brainchild of Secretary of Defense Robert McNamara, used CIA

recon, and parachute pathfinders, who were tasked with locating appropriate landing zones for airborne troops.

The new unit took only the best troops. Selection processes included long and demanding runs and swimming tests, as well as psychological tests to determine how candidates performed under stressful circumstances. The lucky 20 percent who were selected for the unit were then trained in reconnaissance, patrolling, SCUBA and airborne operations, demolition, and escape and evasion. The rigorous training included runs of up to 18 miles, a swim to the surface from a submerged submarine, and eight-mile swims.

By the early 1960s, the Navy had formed the SEALs, and Marine commanders watched helplessly as Force Recon lost its near-monopoly on maritime/land operations. The predecessors to the SEALs, the UDTs (Underwater Demolition Teams) had not strayed too far from the water. The SEALs however, operated on land and sea, and also conducted airborne missions. Needless to say, the Marine hierarchy was not pleased. U.S. Marines have never quite been convinced of the aptitude of Navy sailors—whether or not they were trained as special operators. The Marine Corps brass also did not understand why

Having made final adjustments to his static line parachute rig and awaiting final inspection by a jumpmaster, a Force Recon Marine and his squad ready to make a jump over Camp Pendleton from a helicopter.

Waiting at the ready with MP-5 weapons and protective gear, Force Recon Marines wait for the blast to open a secured door during a live-fire room-clearance exercise. This scenario includes rescuing two hostages and suppressing enemy forces controlling the building. As the post–Cold War era changes, exercises such as these have become more frequent.

Firing from a prone position, Force Recon Marines fire at targets from close range with MP-5 weapons. They must requalify routinely on each of the weapons they operate. With the MP-5, these Marines will shoot from various ranges and shooting positions and must achieve a passing score in each area.

operatives as well as members from Force Recon, the SEALs, Special Forces, and Air Force commandos to launch raids into North Vietnam, Laos, and Cambodia.

Members of the group also served as advisors to Montagnard units which were trained in counterinsurgency and unconventional warfare tactics. The SOG also recruited and taught agents to organize resistance movements inside North Vietnam; conducted kidnappings and assassinations of key cadres; and led attempted POW rescues. The group's members wore civilian clothes or enemy uniforms to conceal the fact that they were U.S. troops. Even after SOG was disbanded, Force Recon worked closely with members of the Special Forces and often went on operations together because of shortages in trained troops. With their regular units, four-man Force Recon patrols were authorized to travel up to 300 miles inland to collect information. It included

Waiting for the command to engage their objective, these Marines stand with their back to the target and MP-5 weapons at the ready. On command, they must turn and shoot their targets in two kill zones within just seconds.

A Marine fires on a target with an MP-5 weapon during training and weapons qualifications at Camp Pendleton. Marines will fire from various distances from the target and be expected to hit the two primary kill zones, the head and chest, from each distance in different firing positions.

A Force Recon marine surveys an area where his squad stops near a road crossing, while on a patrol training mission. Members of Special Operations teams, like the Marines Force Recon, are often used in small numbers as forward reconnaissance personnel and a lone source of human intelligence (HUMINT) collection, the most reliable source of information.

Fast roping down from a helicopter, Force Recon Marines practice their techniques on the Force Recon compound at Camp Pendleton in California. Fast roping is a quick means of insertion used by military forces throughout the world, conventional and special operations alike.

Covering their points of fire, Force Recon soldiers arrange themselves symmetrically to cover all views around a 360-degree area. This method is used when a team initially stops for any duration to insure the security of the area and enable a quick response if fired upon.

As part of a four-man patrol, a Force Recon marine spreads out over an area the patrol plans to secure. Although not part of U.S. Special Operations Command, Force Recon members are trained to do most of what the other Special Operations Forces can do—and some they cannot. As is true with SEALs, they conduct amphibious missions and ship and oil platform takedowns. Similar to the Rangers, they often fight in small units, are airborne qualified, and train in a variety of climates. And like Special Forces and Delta, their mission statement includes conducting special reconnaissance and counterterrorism operations.

Advancing with a wave to the shoreline, a Marine Force Recon boat leader gives the closed fist sign telling the coxswain, the boat's driver, to shut off power to the outboard engine. This maneuver is practiced repeatedly by all Special Operations teams who use the water and the CRRC as a method of coming ashore. The maneuver must be done with a great deal of precision for the advance to work properly.

data on the number of enemy forces, locations of camps, and their weapons capability. If the Force Recon teams encountered small enemy units, they would usually set up an ambush site. The missions typically lasted five or six days.

In Vietnam, the recon teams rarely did airborne drops, and instead relied heavily on helicopter insertion and extraction. They rarely performed aquatic reconnaissance, leaving that to UDT and SEAL teams. Meanwhile, Battalion Recon teams of up to eight Marines concentrated on short-range operations. Throughout the war, there were as many as 40 teams on the ground at all times.

In 1991, Force Recon companies saw extensive duty. During Operation Desert Storm when the 1st Reconnaissance Company was the first ground unit launched into Kuwait.

Force Recon units have conducted surveillance and helped provide security during the U.S. withdrawal in Somalia, and assisted in the United Nations blockades against Iraq and Serbia.

Force Recon Marines survey an area at Camp Pendleton as they conduct a patrol and reconnaissance training mission. Force Recon members conduct amphibious reconnaissance, deep ground reconnaissance, surveillance, recovery of sensitive materials, hostage rescues, raids and unconventional warfare in support of Marine Expeditionary Forces, and task forces, including joint operations with other Special Operations units.

CHAPTER SIX

THE FUTURE OF SPECIAL OPERATIONS

With the passing of each major military conflict, starting with World War II, America's Special Operations units have been defunded or disbanded. After the Vietnam War, the units were not returned to full strength until after the failed Iranian hostage rescue at Desert One in 1980. Because the fallout from that disaster is still fresh in the minds of congressional representatives, it is unlikely that any significant cuts will take place in the near future. Indeed, even as military budgets continue to shrink since the dissolution of the Soviet Union and the communist bloc, Congress has continued to fund Special Operations Forces.

While lessons from the failed Iran hostage rescue provide perhaps the most important reason for the nation's strong Special Operations community, other practical reasons make signigicant changes in the forces unlikely in the near future. First, while the American people may have doubts about low-intensity warfare, that type of warfare is preferable to large-scale involvement. The use of SOF is a way for the United States to exert itself without risking the lives of thousands of young military men and women in a conflict halfway around the world. As long as American political leaders feel the need to provide a visible forward presence, the nation will need Special Operations units. And, unfortunately, there will likely be more El Salvadors and Panamas and Somalias in America's future. It is unlikely, however, that there will be another Vietnam.

One of the areas of Special Operations likely to experience the greatest growth is the training of other nations' forces in foreign internal defense (FID) and coalition support. While FID has long been one of the primary missions of Army Special Forces, other SOF units are beginning to expand their own training capabilities in light of a heavier emphasis on coalition warfare. The Air Force Special Operations Command (AFSOC) reactivated the 6th Special Operation Squadron

Silhouetted by the sun, a Marine Force Recon soldier walks through a brush-shrouded valley on a patrol mission. The various terrain at Camp Pendleton in California offers Marines the chance to train in jungle, desert, and coastal environments.

at Eglin Air Force Base in 1994 to train foreign aviation units in foreign internal defense, unconventional warfare, and coalition support. The squadron will be at full strength by 1998 and focus on training allied air forces, primarily in the Middle East, Asia, and Latin America.

Finally, the threat of terrorism and the continuing menace of organized drug operations will also keep the Special Operations community busy. In the wake of the attack on U.S. facilities in Saudi Arabia in 1996, the forward deployment of SOF units to potential trouble spots in the Middle East and South and Central America will likely be expanded.

The ways in which the conventional wars of the future are fought will also heavily influence the future of special operatives. As the trend of attempting to limit casualties in war continues, USSOCOM's "Quiet Professionals" will be in the forefront. Psychological warfare—perhaps the oldest form of warfare—is also likely to receive a more prominent role on the battlefield of the next century. During Operation Desert Storm, some 650 PSYOP specialists were dispatched to Saudi Arabia. By war's end, the operators had broadcast radio messages and printed and dropped 29 million leaflets on Iraqi soldiers in Kuwait. Shaken by the messages threatening impending invasion and questions of whether the troops really wanted to die for their leader, thousands of Iraqis surrendered, saving not only thousands of Iraqis, but also untold numbers of potential coalition casualties. In the future, as psychological tactics become more sophisticated, PSYOP operatives might be able to allow forces to avoid war altogether.

The weapons of the next century are also likely to focus on causing fewer deaths. One of the reasons for this is that special operators are often called to perform missions in crowded quarters when the target is surrounded by innocents. Such weapons, generally called nonlethal incapacitators, could range from stun guns to a hand-held laser weapon that would take out an enemy with far less unintended casualties than caused by a conventional weapon.

The nation's military-industrial complex spends billions of dollars each year developing—and attempting to sell—new weapons system. For the special operations arena, USSOCOM contributes the Special Operations Research, Development, and Acquisition Center (SORDAC), and the Army offers the Concepts and Studies Division (CSD), which dreams up futuristic devices at the Army's Special Warfare Center. Some of the most frequently mentioned ideas include uniforms conditioned with anti-fungal chemicals and extra ballistic protection that will allow troops to keep their clothes clean and make the soldiers a bit more bulletproof. Such technology would save lives and allow special operators to haul lighter loads.

Special Operations forces of the future could also be given a "sensory enhancement pill" that would allow them to see and remember every detail on their reconnaissance missions. They could be further aided by special headgear fitted with infrared, radar, and microwave detectors that would display everything through goggles worn over the eyes. In their rucksacks would be microprocessors and modems with detailed information about their objective and medical advice that team medics could use to treat the seriously wounded. Plugged in the ear of each commando might be a sound amplification device so they can hear the sounds around them better.

The bottom line, however, is that no matter what advances are made in technology, it will be the special operator—"The Quiet Professional"—the soldier behind the machines, who stands ready to answer the call.

INDEX